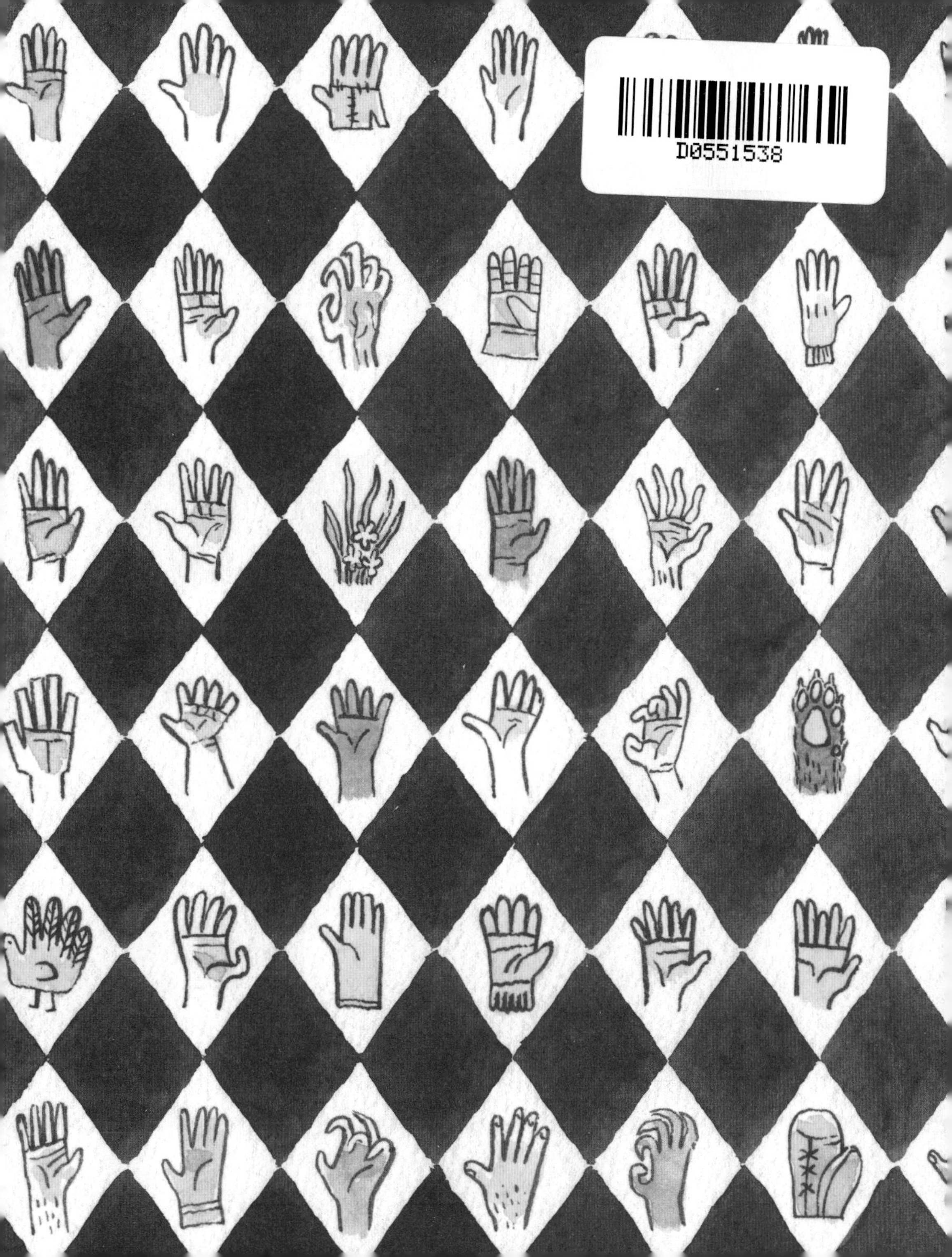

THE CREEPS

A DEEP DARK FEARS COLLECTION

FRAN KRAUSE

TEN SPEED PRESS

CALIFORNIA | NEW YORK

INTRODUCTION

OH, HELLO! THANKS FOR PICKING UP THIS BOOK!

IT'S KINDA SCARY.

WE SHOULD PROBABLY PREPARE A BIT BEFORE WE READ IT.

LET'S START BY NAILING ALL OUR WINDOWS SHUT.

THAT OUGHT TO KEEP OUT MOST OF THE MONSTERS.

ALSO, YOU SHOULD PROBABLY TELL THE GHOSTS IN YOUR ATTIC...

...TO KEEP QUIET FOR THE NEXT FEW HOURS.

ALL RIGHT, I THINK THAT'S
EVERYTHING. I HOPE YOU—

HEY, CAT CAT, GET
OUT OF MY CHIPS!

AHEM...

I HOPE YOU ENJOY
THIS BOOK!

FEAR #1

WHEN I READ BY MYSELF, I READ OUT LOUD,

IN CASE THERE ARE ANY CURIOUS GHOSTS OR SPIRITS NEARBY.

FEAR # 2

SOMETIMES WHEN I SAY
OR DO SOMETHING AWKWARD,

I FEEL LIKE I'M NOT
REALLY HUMAN.

I'M JUST AN ANIMAL HOOKED
UP TO A HUMAN SIMULATOR,

SURROUNDED BY A GROUP
OF DISAPPOINTED SCIENTISTS.

FEAR #3

WHEN I'M USING A PUBLIC BATHROOM,

SOMETIMES I WONDER IF I'M ALONE.

I WORRY IF I PEEK UNDER THE DIVIDER,

I'LL MAKE EYE CONTACT.

FRAN KRAUSE

FEAR #4

MY KITCHEN HAS A BLACK
& WHITE CHECKERED FLOOR.

WHEN I GO IN THERE
LATE AT NIGHT,

I ONLY STEP ON THE
WHITE TILES,

BECAUSE IT LOOKS LIKE I'D
FALL THROUGH THE OTHERS.

FRAN KRAUSE

FEAR #5

WHENEVER I'M INVITED TO A PARTY,

I WORRY I'LL BE THE ONLY PERSON TO SHOW,

BECAUSE IT WAS ALL SOMEONE'S JOKE.

FEAR #6

IF YOU EVER SNEEZE WITHOUT CLOSING YOUR EYES,

YOUR EYEBALLS WILL POP OUT OF YOUR HEAD.

FEAR #7

WHEN ANIMALS ARE ACTING VERY NICE TO ME,

I WORRY THAT THEY HAVE AN EXTRA SENSE,

AND THEY'RE JUST TREATING ME EXTRA-NICE

BECAUSE THEY KNOW I'M GOING TO DIE SOON.

FEAR #8

YOU LEAVE A TRAIL OF
STRING EVERYWHERE YOU GO.

WHEN YOU DIE, IT PULLS YOUR
SPIRIT INTO THE AFTERLIFE.

UNLESS IT GETS TANGLED,

AND YOUR GHOST IS LEFT TO HAUNT THE KNOTS.

FEAR #9

MY MOTHER'S OFFICE WAS
UP A TALL, ECHOING STAIRWELL.

I COULD NEVER TELL IF
THE SOUNDS I HEARD

WERE ECHOES OF MY
OWN FOOTSTEPS

OR A SIGN THAT I WAS
BEING FOLLOWED.

FEAR #10

I CAN'T EAT CHICKEN LEGS,

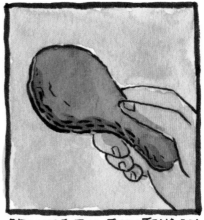

BECAUSE THE THIN TENDON IN ITS ANKLE

REMINDS ME OF MY OWN

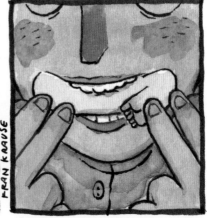

AND MAKES ME FEEL LIKE A CANNIBAL.

FEAR #11

AN ABANDONED FACTORY WAS ON OUR WALK HOME.

ON THE TOP FLOOR, WE SAW A GIRL AT THE CORNER WINDOW.

WE SNUCK INSIDE, BUT UP IN THE TOP CORNER ROOM,

THERE WAS NO WINDOW AT ALL.

FEAR #12

WHEN I WAS A KID, MY DAD WOULD COOK DELICIOUS PORK.

I ASKED HIM, "WHAT IS THE STEAM RISING FROM THE PAN?"

HE TOLD ME:

"THAT'S THE PIG'S GHOST."

FEAR #13

WHEN I DO SOMETHING STUPID AND ALMOST GET KILLED, I WORRY I JUST KILLED ANOTHER VERSION OF MYSELF IN AN ALTERNATE UNIVERSE.

I WORRY I JUST KILLED ANOTHER VERSION OF MYSELF IN AN ALTERNATE UNIVERSE.

I WORRY I JUST KILLED ANOTHER VERSION OF MYSELF IN AN ALTERNATE UNIVERSE.

FEAR # 14

IF I FALL ASLEEP

WITH MY ARM HANGING OFF MY BED,

SOMETHING UNDER THE BED

HOLDS MY HAND WHILE I SLEEP.

FEAR # 15

WHEN I'M TALKING WITH
A COMPUTER VOICE,

SOMETIMES I FEEL LIKE
IT'S LISTENING,

AND IT'S ALIVE SOMEWHERE, AND IT'LL TURN AGAINST ME.

FEAR # 16

I'M AFRAID THAT WHEN I
FALL IN THE SHOWER,

I'LL BE KNOCKED
UNCONSCIOUS,

MY LONG HAIR WILL
STOP THE DRAIN,

AND THE TUB WILL FILL
WITH ME AT THE BOTTOM.

FEAR # 17

WHEN YOU GO TO SLEEP, NEVER LEAVE YOUR SHOES BY A WINDOW. NEVER POINT THEM TOWARD YOUR BED.

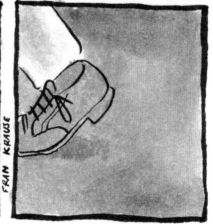

GHOSTS WILL SEE THAT AS AN INVITATION TO STEP INSIDE.

FEAR #18

WHEN I DRIVE HOME, I'm SO TIRED

I FEEL LIKE I'M ON AUTOPILOT.

I WORRY I'LL MISS my TURN,

AND I'LL WIND UP FAR FROM HOME.

FRAN KRAUSE

FEAR #19

WHEN I FEED THE BIRDS IN THE PARK,

I TRY TO THROW THE BREAD FAR AWAY FROM ME.

I DON'T WANT THE BIRDS
TO SWARM ME

AND, IN THE CONFUSION,
MISTAKE ME FOR BREAD.

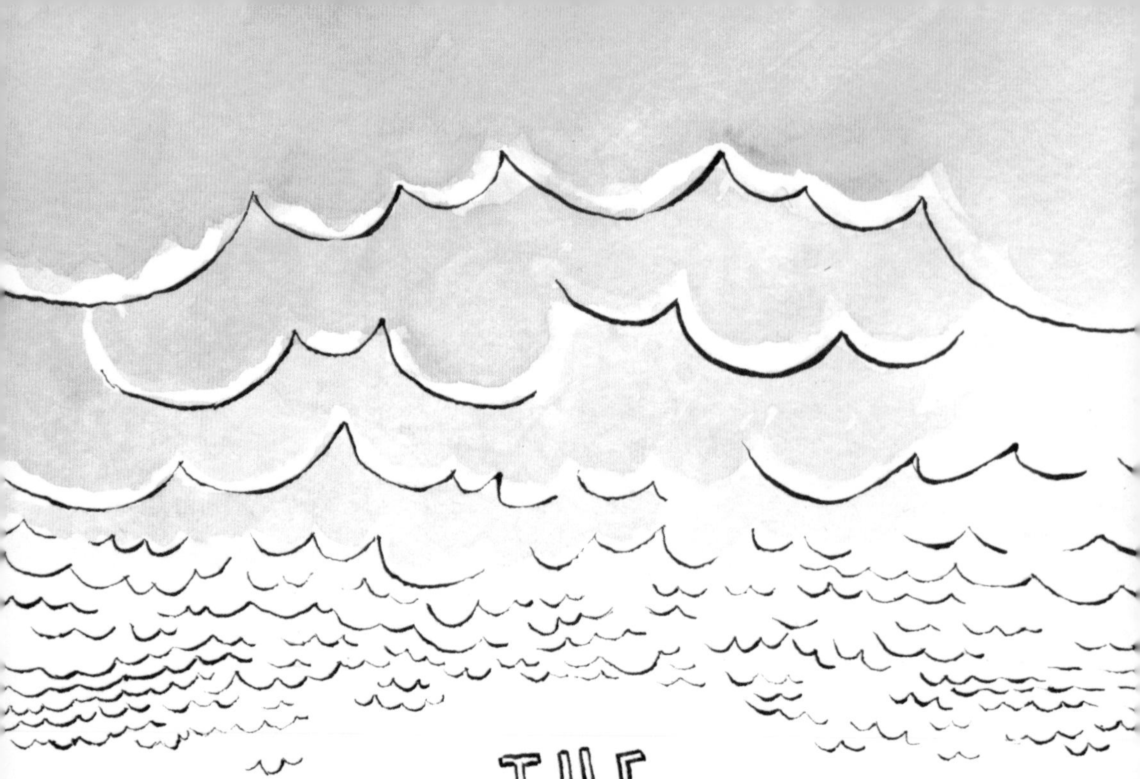

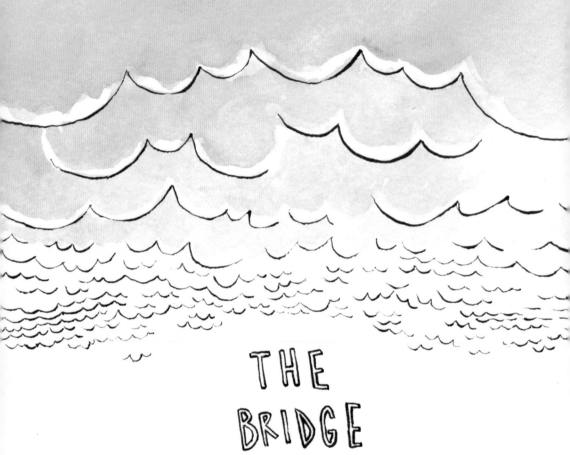

THE BRIDGE

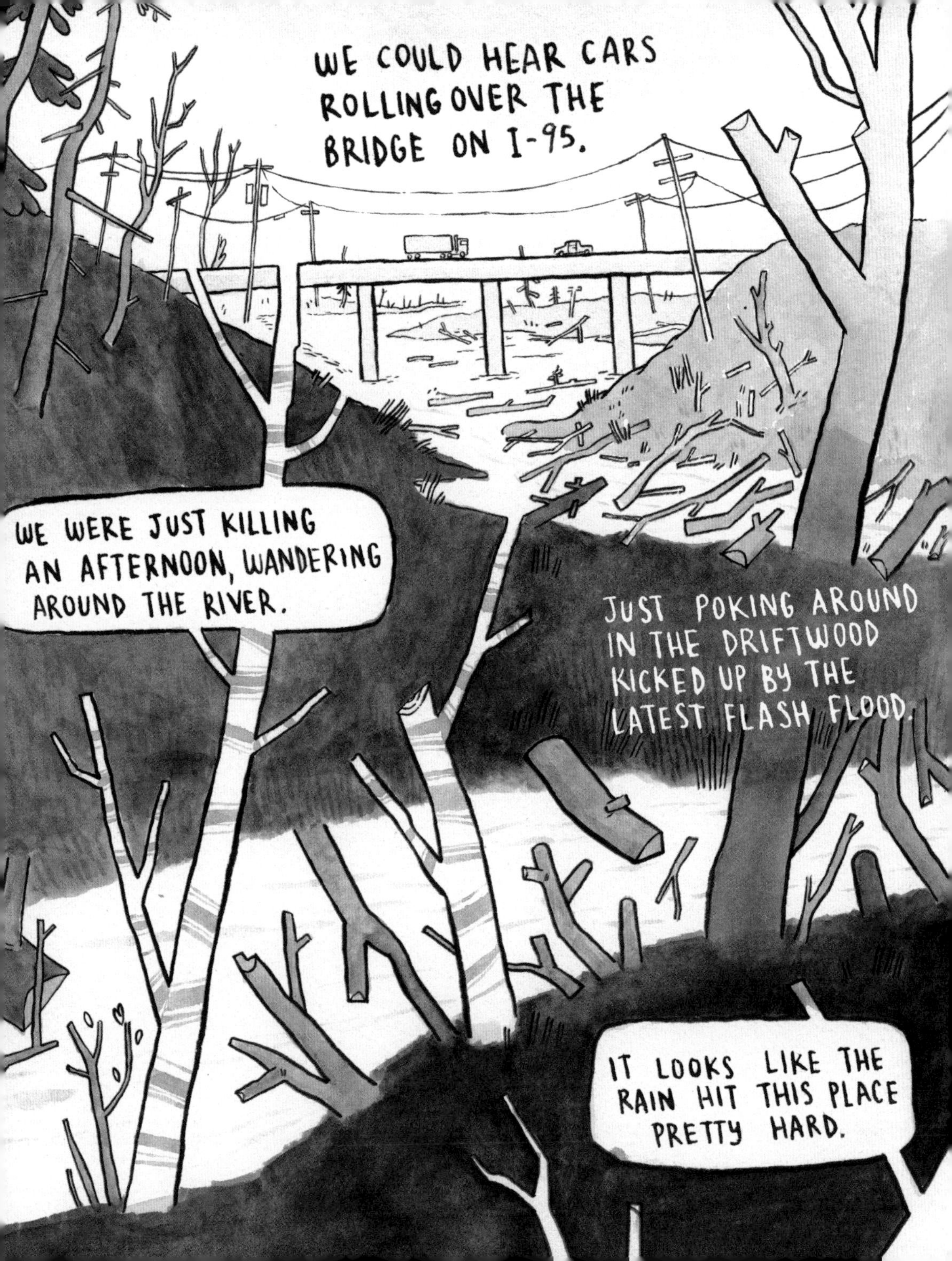
WE COULD HEAR CARS ROLLING OVER THE BRIDGE ON I-95.
WE WERE JUST KILLING AN AFTERNOON, WANDERING AROUND THE RIVER.
JUST POKING AROUND IN THE DRIFTWOOD KICKED UP BY THE LATEST FLASH FLOOD.
IT LOOKS LIKE THE RAIN HIT THIS PLACE PRETTY HARD.

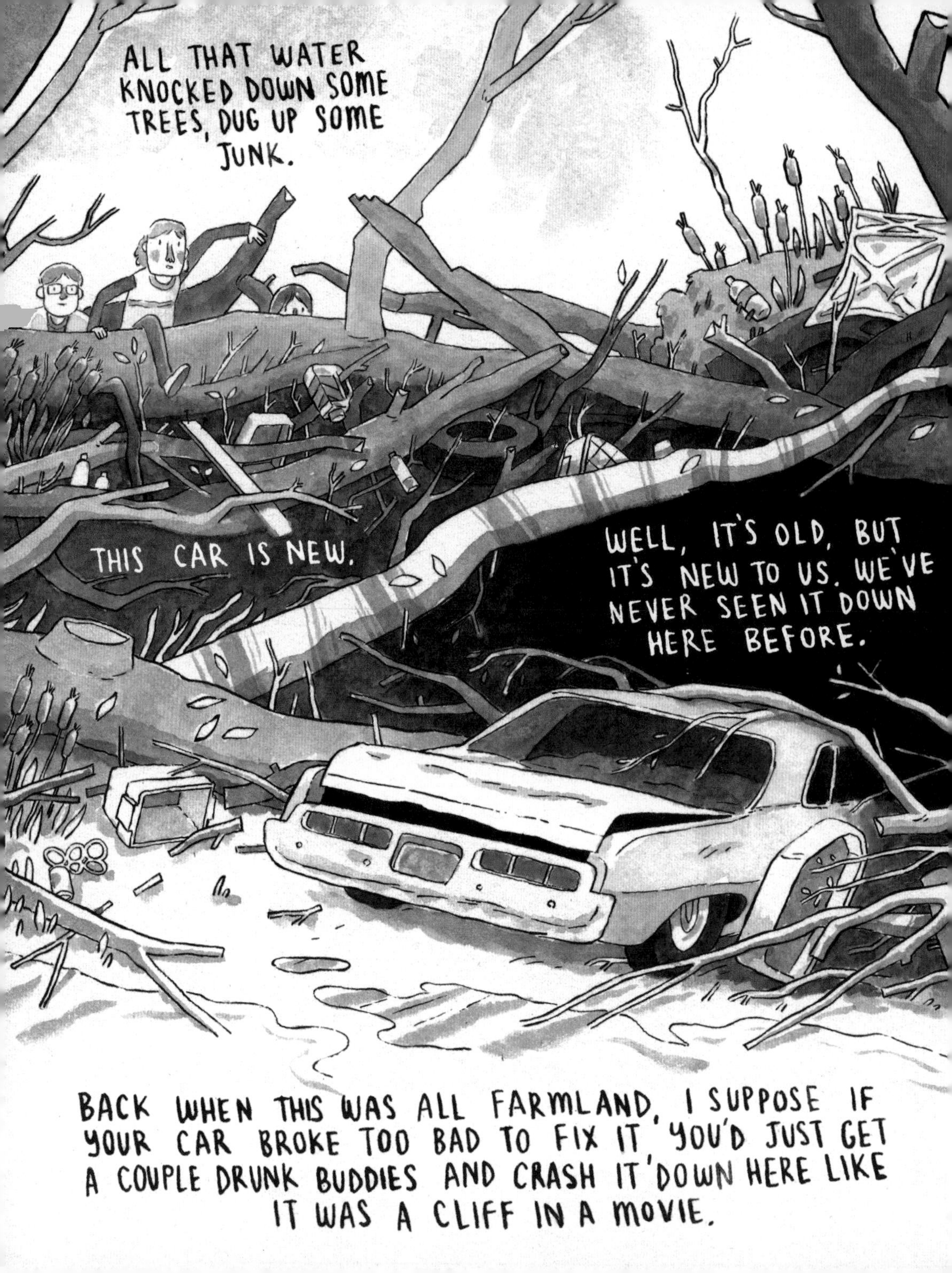
ALL THAT WATER KNOCKED DOWN SOME TREES, DUG UP SOME JUNK.
THIS CAR IS NEW.
WELL, IT'S OLD, BUT IT'S NEW TO US. WE'VE NEVER SEEN IT DOWN HERE BEFORE.
BACK WHEN THIS WAS ALL FARMLAND, I SUPPOSE IF YOUR CAR BROKE TOO BAD TO FIX IT, YOU'D JUST GET A COUPLE DRUNK BUDDIES AND CRASH IT DOWN HERE LIKE IT WAS A CLIFF IN A MOVIE.

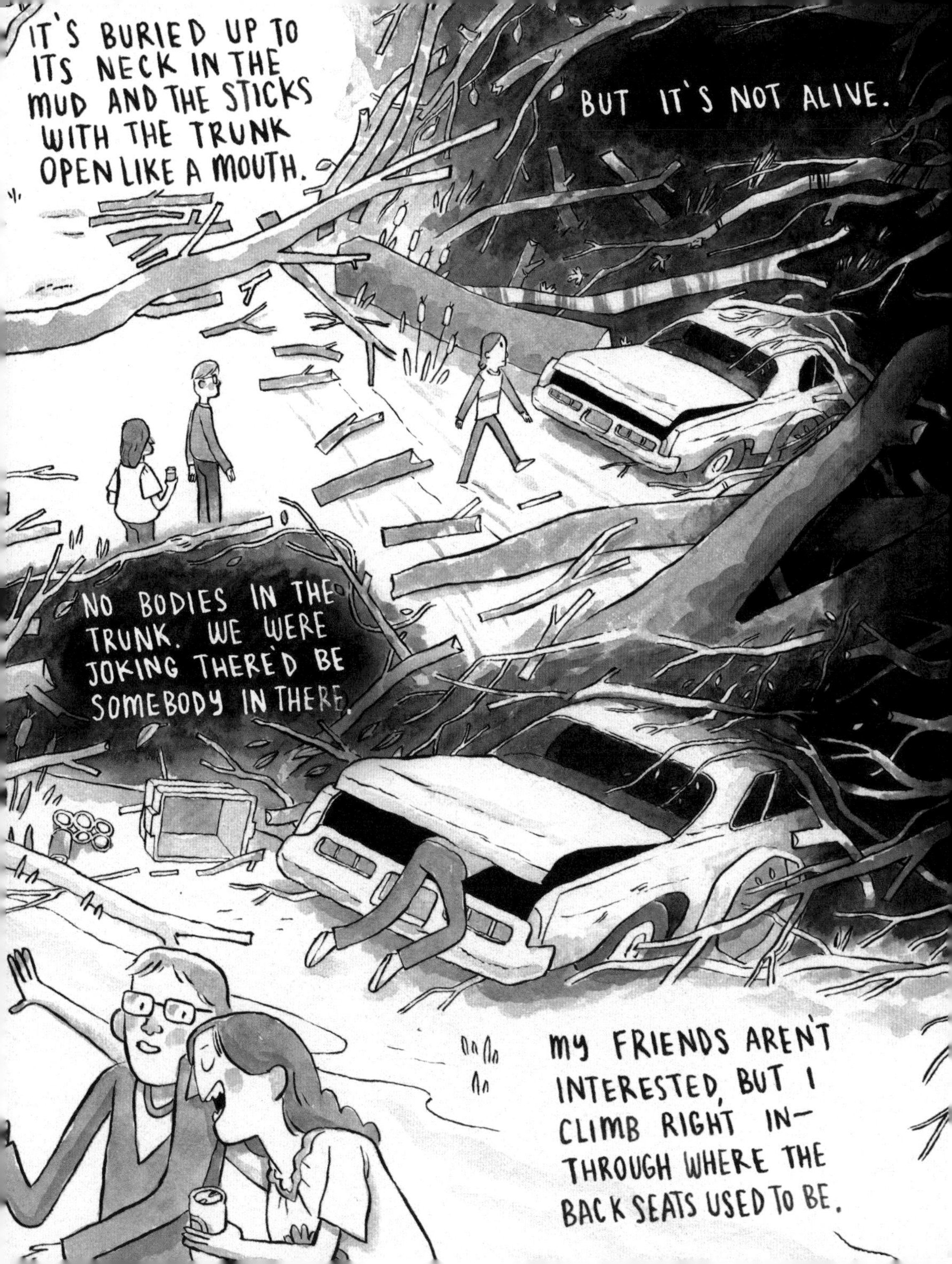
IT'S BURIED UP TO ITS NECK IN THE MUD AND THE STICKS WITH THE TRUNK OPEN LIKE A MOUTH.
BUT IT'S NOT ALIVE.
NO BODIES IN THE TRUNK. WE WERE JOKING THERE'D BE SOMEBODY IN THERE.
MY FRIENDS AREN'T INTERESTED, BUT I CLIMB RIGHT IN— THROUGH WHERE THE BACK SEATS USED TO BE.

IT SMELLS LIKE A
BASEMENT.

I CAN'T BELIEVE THIS
THING USED TO GO
EIGHTY MILES AN HOUR
DOWN THE THRUWAY.

AFTER A WHILE, MY EYES
ADJUST TO THE DARK.

THROUGH THE WINDSHIELD,
IT ALMOST LOOKS LIKE
THERE ARE LIGHTS.

LITTLE SPOTS, PROBABLY JUST
DIM REFLECTIONS, LIKE MILE
MARKERS ALONG THE ROAD.

IT'S PROBABLY JUST THE TRAFFIC ON THE BRIDGE, BUT I THINK I CAN ALMOST HEAR THE RUSH OF THE ROAD.

IT WOULD HAVE BEEN LOUD IN AN OLD CAR LIKE THIS.

WISH I COULD ROLL DOWN ...E WINDOWS AND FEEL THE BREEZE.

BUT IT'S TOO DARK IN HERE. I WOULDN'T BE ABLE TO FIND THE HANDLE.

IT FEELS WEIRD IN HERE, LIKE SOMEONE'S SITTING NEXT TO ME.

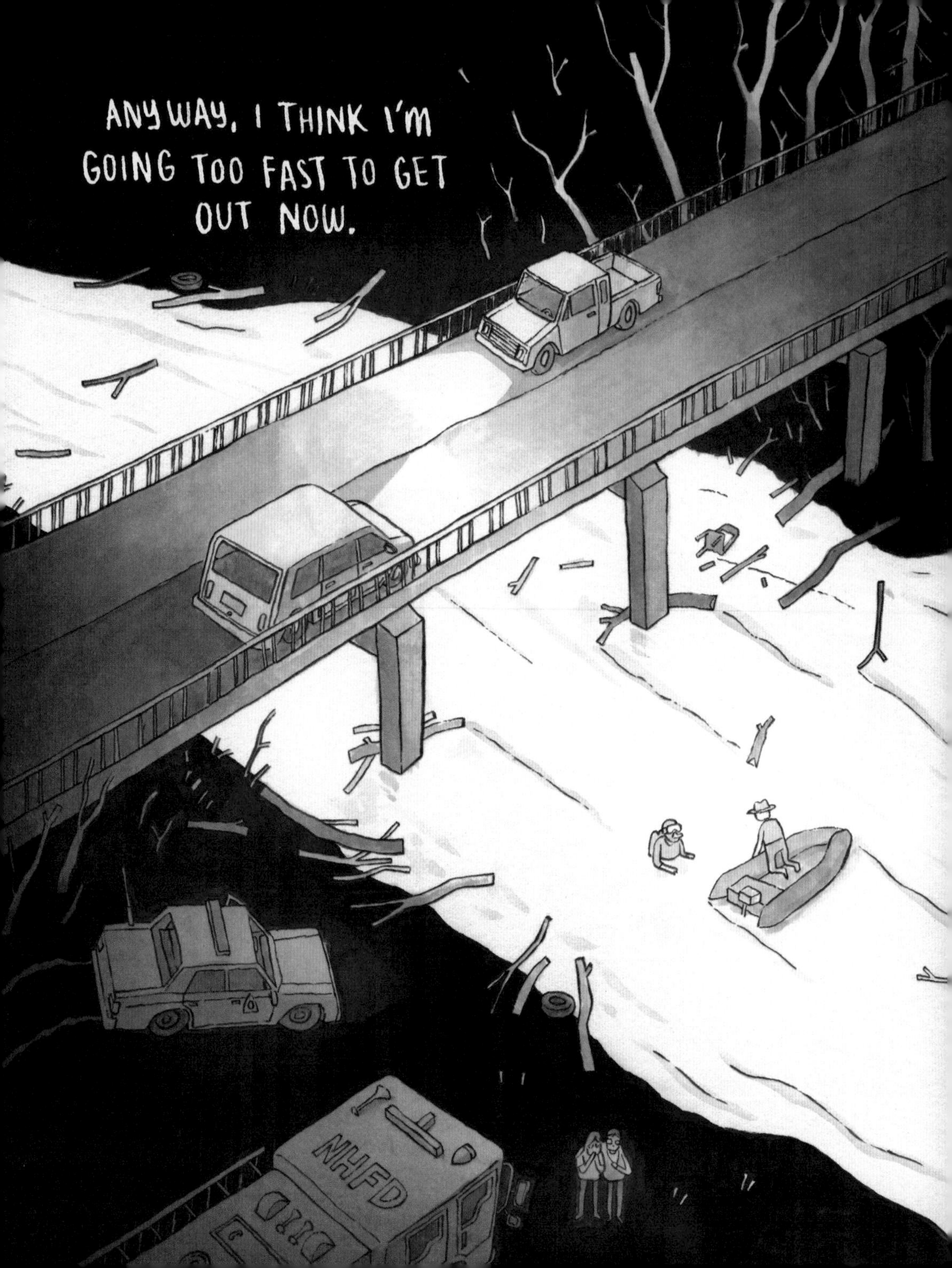
ANYWAY, I THINK I'M GOING TOO FAST TO GET OUT NOW.
NHFD

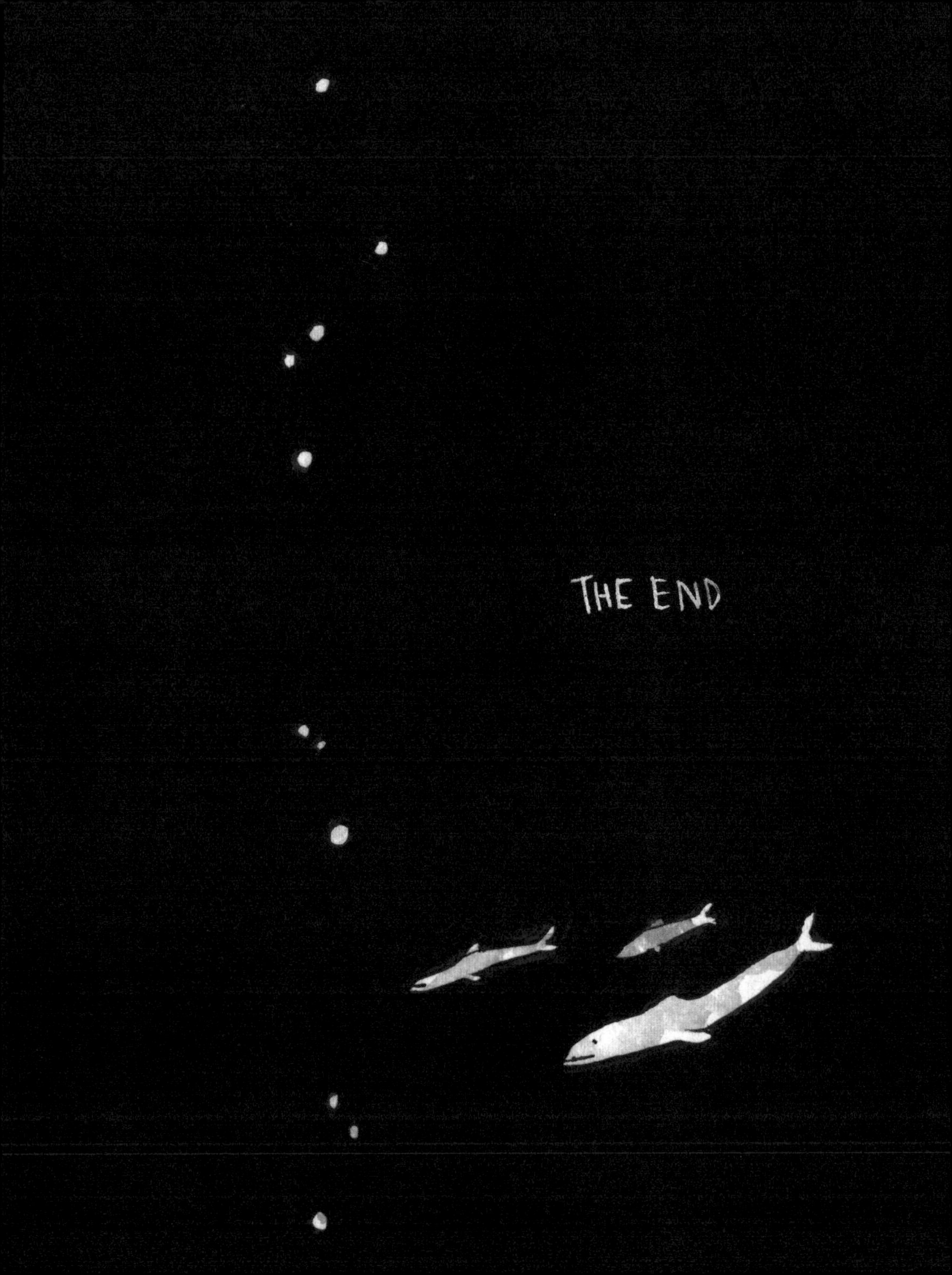
THE END

FEAR #20

WHENEVER I CLEAN
OUT MY POCKETS,

I WORRY THAT I'LL
THROW SOMETHING OUT,

AND THE NEXT DAY
I'LL FIND OUT

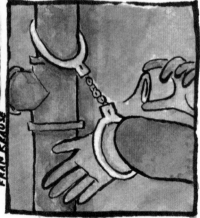

THAT I THREW OUT
SOMETHING USEFUL.

FEAR #21

WE EACH TRIED TO DRAW
SOMETHING REALLY SCARY.

I MADE A LADY THAT
GAVE US BOTH NIGHTMARES.

I FELT LIKE I'D MADE
SOMETHING EVIL, SO WE
BURNED THE DRAWING.

I KNEW SHE COULDN'T
COME BACK WITHOUT
A DRAWING SOMEWHERE.

FEAR # 22

WHEN I WATCH SOMEONE
DO SOMETHING MOMENTOUS,

I'M AFRAID IF I BECOME
TOO INVOLVED,

WE'LL SWITCH PLACES

AND I'LL MESS IT ALL UP.

FEAR #23

MY PARENTS LIVE
FAR AWAY.

WHEN OUR PHONE CALLS
ARE INTERRUPTED,

I WORRY THAT A NUCLEAR
BOMB HAS DESTROYED
THEIR TOWN,

AND THE SHOCK WAVE IS
HEADED MY WAY.

FEAR #24

I LIKE TO STAY UP
LATE ON MY PHONE,

BUT THE LIGHT IS
SO BRIGHT.

EVERYTHING ELSE IN
MY ROOM

IS HIDDEN IN DARKNESS.

FEAR #25

MY FRIEND TOLD ME IF I HIDE UNDER MY SHEETS,

WHEN I OPEN MY EYES, I'LL FIND SOMETHING WAITING.

FEAR #26

WHEN STUFFED ANIMALS
ARE MADE,

THEY'RE LIVING, BREATHING
CREATURES—

BUT THEY SUFFOCATE IN
THEIR PACKAGING,

AND WE PLAY WITH THEIR
LIFELESS BODIES.

FEAR #27

 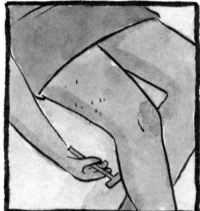

WHEN I'M SHAVING MY LEGS,

AND I GET TO THE TIGHT TENDON BEHIND MY KNEE,

FRAN KRAUSE

I WORRY I'LL NICK IT WITH MY RAZOR,

AND THE MUSCLE WILL ROLL UP LIKE A WINDOWSHADE.

FEAR # 28

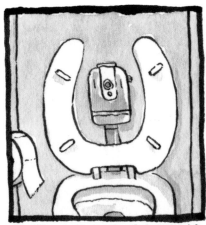

THERE ARE SECRET CAMERAS IN AUTOMATIC-FLUSH TOILETS.
WHENEVER I SEE ONE,

I MAKE SURE THE PERSON WATCHING THROUGH THE
CAMERA KNOWS I'M WISE TO THEIR CONSPIRACY.

FEAR #29

SINCE MY DAD DIED,   I WORRY THAT HE HAUNTS
THE HOUSE WHERE WE GREW UP,

BUT SINCE WE MOVED AWAY, HE HAS TO LIVE WITH STRANGERS.

FEAR #30

I WAS AFRAID OF LOSING MY SOUL TO THE DEVIL,

SO I MADE A TITLE AND HID IT CAREFULLY.

YEARS LATER, I HAVE NO IDEA WHERE IT IS.

I HAVE NO IDEA WHO OWNS MY SOUL.

FEAR #31

SOMETIMES IT FEELS LIKE THE WORLD IS A VIDEO GAME,

AND EVERYTHING I SEE IS RENDERED BY COMPUTERS.

IF I COULD ONLY TURN MY HEAD FAST ENOUGH,

I COULD CATCH THE BLANK LANDSCAPE BEFORE IT LOADS.

FEAR #32

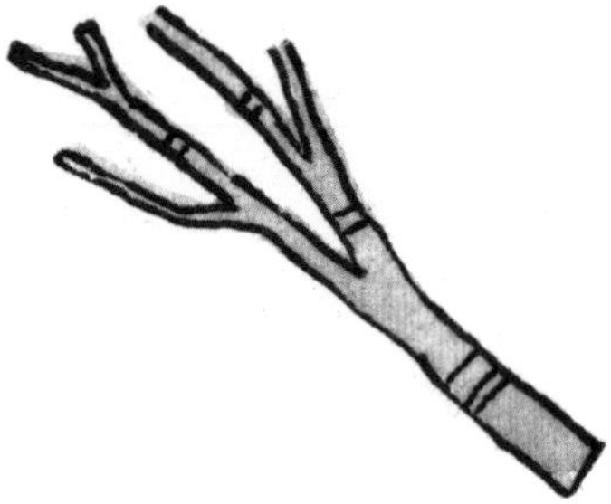

THERE ARE TREES ALL AROUND MY HOUSE, SO I TRY
TO SLEEP IN A PLACE WHERE I'LL BE SAFE IF THEY FALL.

FEAR #33

I WAS REALLY DEPRESSED, SO I GOT DRUNK & PASSED OUT IN THE WOODS.

EVER SINCE THEN, MY LIFE HAS BEEN REALLY HAPPY.

SOMETIMES I WORRY I DIED THAT NIGHT,

AND I'M ACTUALLY IN MY AFTERLIFE.

FEAR #34

MY VACUUM CLEANER MAKES A LOT OF NOISE.

SOMETIMES, IF I LISTEN CLOSELY,

I THINK I HEAR VOICES IN THE STATIC,

AND I FEEL LIKE SOME-THING IS SNEAKING UP ON ME.

FEAR #35

I AM FIVE FEET TALL.
WHEN I'm AT THE SUBWAY,

I ALWAYS WAIT AT LEAST
SIX FEET FROM THE TRACKS.

THAT WAY, IF ANYONE
TRIES TO KILL ME,

I'LL FALL SHORT.

FEAR # 36

EARLY IN THE WOMB,

ONE TWIN SOMETIMES ABSORBS THE OTHER.

WHEN MY KIDS' ROOM GOES QUIET,

I WORRY IT MIGHT HAVE FINALLY HAPPENED.

FEAR # 37

WHEN I'M OUTDOORS WITH MY EASEL,

GETTING LOST IN THE SCENERY,

I'LL FEEL THIRSTY,

AND I'LL ACCIDENTALLY DRINK MY TURPENTINE.

FEAR # 38

THE LIGHT WAS BROKEN
IN THE GUEST ROOM.

ON THE WALL WAS A
PAINTING OF A FACE.

I BARELY SLEPT. THE
NEXT MORNING, I SAW...

...THE PAINTING WAS
ACTUALLY A WINDOW.

FEAR # 39

I CAN'T STAND HAVING MY BLOOD DRAWN.

PARTLY BECAUSE I'M SCARED OF NEEDLES,

BUT MOSTLY, FOR DAYS AFTER, I FEAR THAT IF I POINT AT ANYTHING,

BLOOD WILL JET FROM MY INNER ELBOW.

FEAR # 40

I NEVER GO TO THE TOILET DURING THUNDERSTORMS,

BECAUSE THE LIGHTNING COULD FOLLOW ANY FLUID

STRAIGHT TO ME.

FEAR # 41

EVERY NIGHT, MY OLDER SISTER TOLD ME A STORY:

MY WHOLE LIFE WAS JUST A HALLUCINATION.

I WAS ACTUALLY JUST A BRAIN IN A JAR,

AND SHE WAS A SCIENTIST WHO FELT SORRY FOR ME AND SENT ME MESSAGES.

FEAR # 42

AFTER DINNER,

MY MOTHER WOULDN'T LET ME SWEEP THE FLOOR,

SO THE DEAD PEOPLE

COULD EAT OUR BREAD CRUMBS AT NIGHT.

FEAR # 43

I'M AFRAID THE GHOST OF MY DOG IS FOLLOWING ME

AND CAN'T FIGURE OUT WHY I'M IGNORING HIM.

FEAR #44

MY GRANDMOTHER TOLD ME
THAT THE WORLD WOULD
END SOMEDAY,

AND ALL GOOD PEOPLE
WOULD BE TELEPORTED
TO HEAVEN.

EVERY TIME I SAW CLOTHES
ON THE GROUND,

I WORRIED MY FAMILY
WAS GONE AND I WAS LEFT
WITH THE BAD PEOPLE.

FEAR #45

WHEN I GO CLIMBING,

I TAKE OFF MY WEDDING RING. IF I FALL,

I DON'T WANT IT TO GET CAUGHT ON A HOLD

AND PULL OFF MY FINGER,

FEAR # 46

I'm LISTENING TO A FAVORITE SONG AND DRIFTING TO SLEEP.

IN MY DREAM, I'M RUNNING HARD TO THE MUSIC'S BEAT,

BUT I GET A STITCH IN MY SIDE AND CAN'T CATCH MY BREATH.

I'LL BE FOUND THE NEXT DAY, CHOKED BY MY HEADPHONE WIRES.

FEAR # 47

IF I NEED TO GET OUT OF BED LATE AT NIGHT,

I SING A LITTLE SONG TO MYSELF.

THAT WAY, I WON'T ACCIDENTALLY SAY ANY MAGIC WORDS

AND SUMMON SPIRITS FROM INSIDE MY MIRROR.

FEAR # 48

PUTTING A SHIRT ON THAT
HAS A SPIDER INSIDE IT.

FEAR # 49

LATE AT NIGHT,

WHEN I SIT CLOSE TO THE
CAMPFIRE,

I WORRY THAT MY
CONTACT LENSES

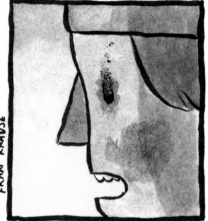

WILL MELT ONTO MY
EYEBALLS.

FEAR #50

WHEN I COME HOME
LATE AT NIGHT,

I KICK MY DOOR OPEN,

SO ANYONE HIDING
BEHIND IT

WILL BE KNOCKED OUT
BEFORE THEY CAN GET ME.

FEAR #51

I HAVEN'T LIKED MASCOT COSTUMES SINCE I WAS A KID.

MY DAD TOOK ME TO A FOOTBALL GAME,

AND HE TOLD ME THEY
WERE EMPTY INSIDE,

UNTIL THEY CAUGHT
A CHILD.

FEAR #52

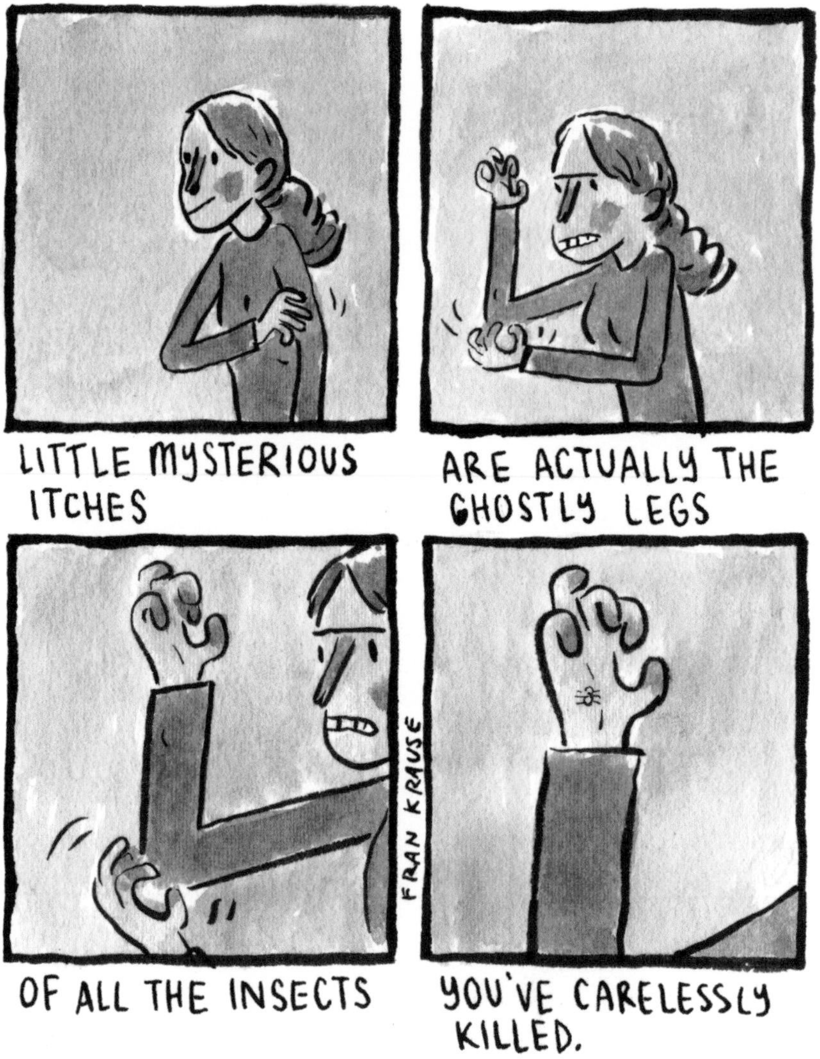
LITTLE MYSTERIOUS ITCHES
ARE ACTUALLY THE GHOSTLY LEGS
OF ALL THE INSECTS
FRAN KRAUSE
YOU'VE CARELESSLY KILLED.

FEAR #83

WHEN SOMEONE DIES, YOU NEED TO COVER UP ALL THEIR MIRRORS.

OTHERWISE, THEIR SPIRIT MAY GET CONFUSED,

AND CRAWL INSIDE THE FRAME,

TRAPPED THERE FOR ALL THEIR AFTERLIFE.

FEAR # 54

I DON'T WANT TO BE LAID TO ETERNAL REST ON MY BACK, DRESSED LIKE I'm GOING TO A JOB INTERVIEW.

PLEASE REMEMBER: I PREFER TO SLEEP ON MY BELLY, DRESSED IN A T-SHIRT AND SWEATPANTS.

FEAR #55

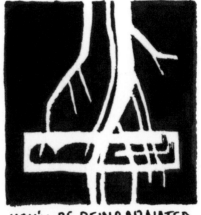

I LIKE TO THINK THAT IF YOU'RE BURIED IN THE GROUND,

YOU'LL BE REINCARNATED AS A TREE OF SOME KIND.

THE STREET I TAKE TO SCHOOL SEPARATES TWO OLD TREES.

THEIR BRANCHES REACH ACROSS. I WONDER WHO THEY WERE.

FRAN KRAUSE

FEAR #56

SOMETIMES I CAN'T HELP BUT WORRY THAT
ANY ONE OF THE RANDOM STRANGERS I PASS

MIGHT BE MY SOUL MATE, AND I'M MISSING
OUR ONLY CHANCE TO EVER MEET.

FEAR #57

WHENEVER I RIDE A
ROLLER COASTER,

I ALWAYS TIE BACK MY
HAIR.

I DON'T WANT IT GETTING
CAUGHT ON ANYTHING.

I MIGHT LOSE MY HEAD.

FEAR #58

SOMETIMES I FEEL LIKE
ALL MY PERSONAL DREAMS,

AND ALL THE GOALS I
HAVE FOR MY LIFE,

ARE ALL TOTALLY BASED
ON FICTIONAL THINGS,

AND NONE OF THEM
WILL EVER COME TRUE.

FEAR # 59

THE THINGS THAT SKIM MY FEET WHILE I'M SWIMMING,
THINGS I BARELY FEEL,

COULD BE DROWNED FINGERTIPS TRYING TO PULL ME UNDER
SO I COULD KEEP THEM COMPANY.

FEAR # 60

SOMETIMES I PRACTICE LYING REALLY FLAT IN BED,

SO I WILL BE SAFE FROM ANY GHOSTS OR MONSTERS.

FEAR #61

I'M AFRAID WHEN I DIE,

MY GHOST WILL BE TETHERED
TO MY CORPSE,

AND I'LL HAVE TO SEE IT
ALL WITHER AWAY,

BEFORE I CAN MOVE ON.

FEAR #62

I WORRY THAT WE ARE AWAKE DURING SURGERY.

WE SEE AND FEEL EVERYTHING.

THE ANESTHETIC ONLY PARALYZES US,

AND WIPES AWAY OUR MEMORIES.

FEAR #63

WHEN I LEAVE MY DRIVEWAY,

I NEED TO WAIT TILL I SEE THE DOOR COMPLETELY CLOSE.

IF I LET MY GUARD DOWN,

SOMEONE MIGHT SLIP IN.

FEAR #64

MY NIGHTMARES FEEL REAL.

I WORRY THAT SOMEDAY,
I'LL SEE SOMETHING ODD,

AND I WON'T KNOW TO BE
AFRAID AND RUN,

BECAUSE I'LL THINK
IT'S ALL A DREAM.

FEAR #65

I WORRY THAT AFTER I DIE,

I'LL BE FORCED TO RELIVE ALL THE LIVES I'VE SPENT

WHILE PLAYING VIDEO GAMES.

I ALWAYS LET MY CHARACTER EAT AND REST OFTEN.

FRAN KRAUSE

FEAR #66

DRIVING LATE AT NIGHT,

I WORRY THE TAILLIGHTS I'M FOLLOWING

BELONG TO A GHOST CAR

THAT WILL LEAD ME OFF A CLIFF.

FEAR #67

I ONCE HAD A DREAM THAT I ATE MY OWN HAND.

THE SKIN AND MUSCLES WERE CHEWY LIKE GUMMY BEARS.

THE BONES WERE BRITTLE AND CRUNCHY LIKE COOKIES.

SINCE THEN, I CAN'T HELP SEEING MY HAND DIFFERENTLY.

FRAN KRAUSE

FEAR #68

WHEN I DON'T READ MY
MESSAGES RIGHT AWAY,

I WORRY MY FRIEND WAS
ASKING FOR HELP...

FROM A KIDNAPPER'S TRUNK.
BUT BY THE TIME I ANSWER,

HER PHONE IS DEAD.

FEAR #69 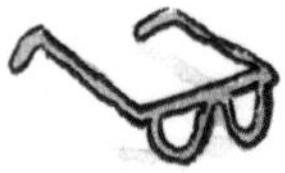

SOMETIMES WHEN THE
SUN IS BRIGHT,

I WORRY MY GLASSES WILL
AMPLIFY THE LIGHT,

LIKE A MAGNIFYING
GLASS CAN DO TO ANTS,

AND I'LL GET TWO HOLES
BURNED THROUGH MY HEAD.

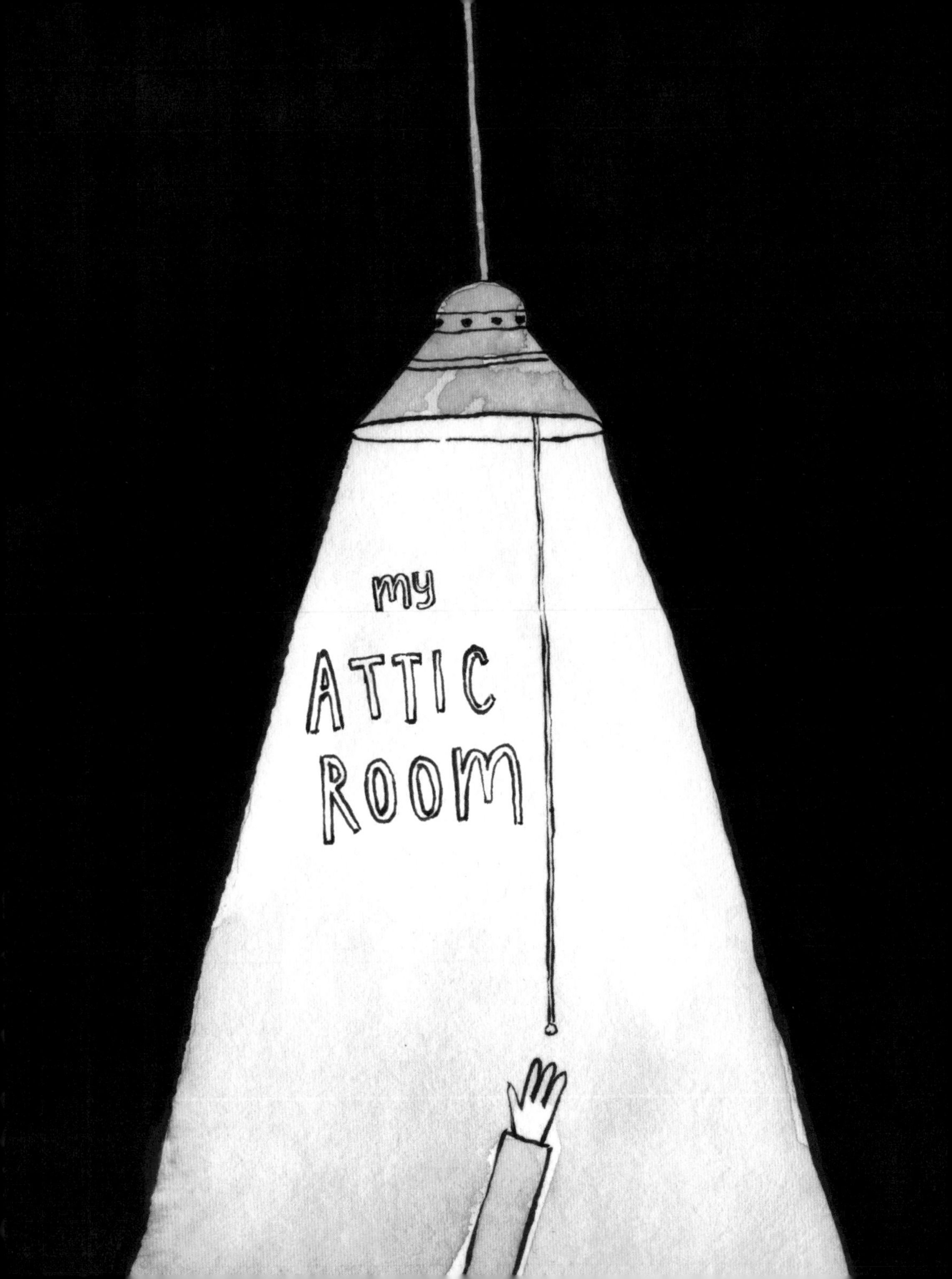
my
ATTIC
ROOM

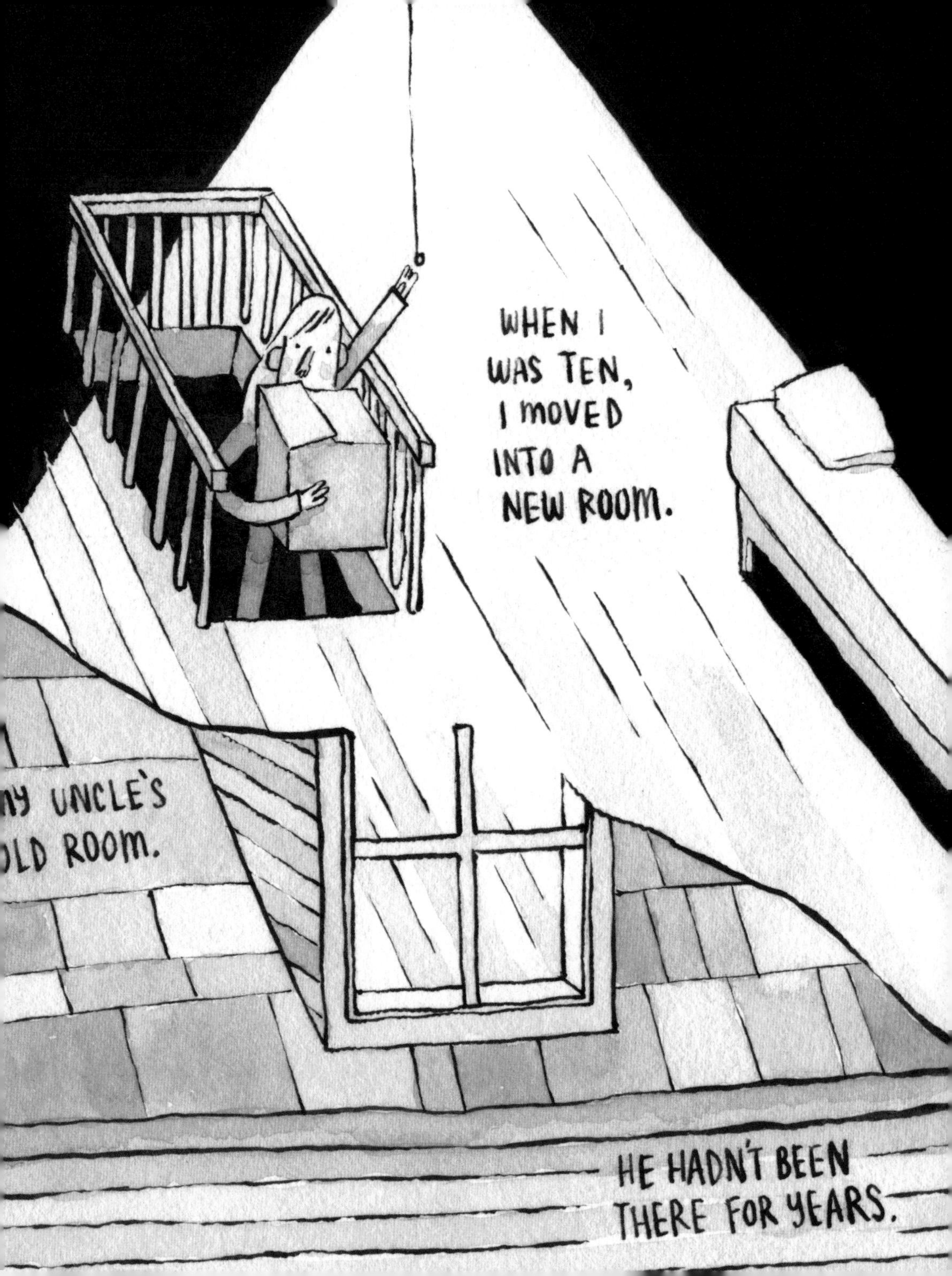
WHEN I WAS TEN, I MOVED INTO A NEW ROOM.
MY UNCLE'S OLD ROOM.
HE HADN'T BEEN THERE FOR YEARS.

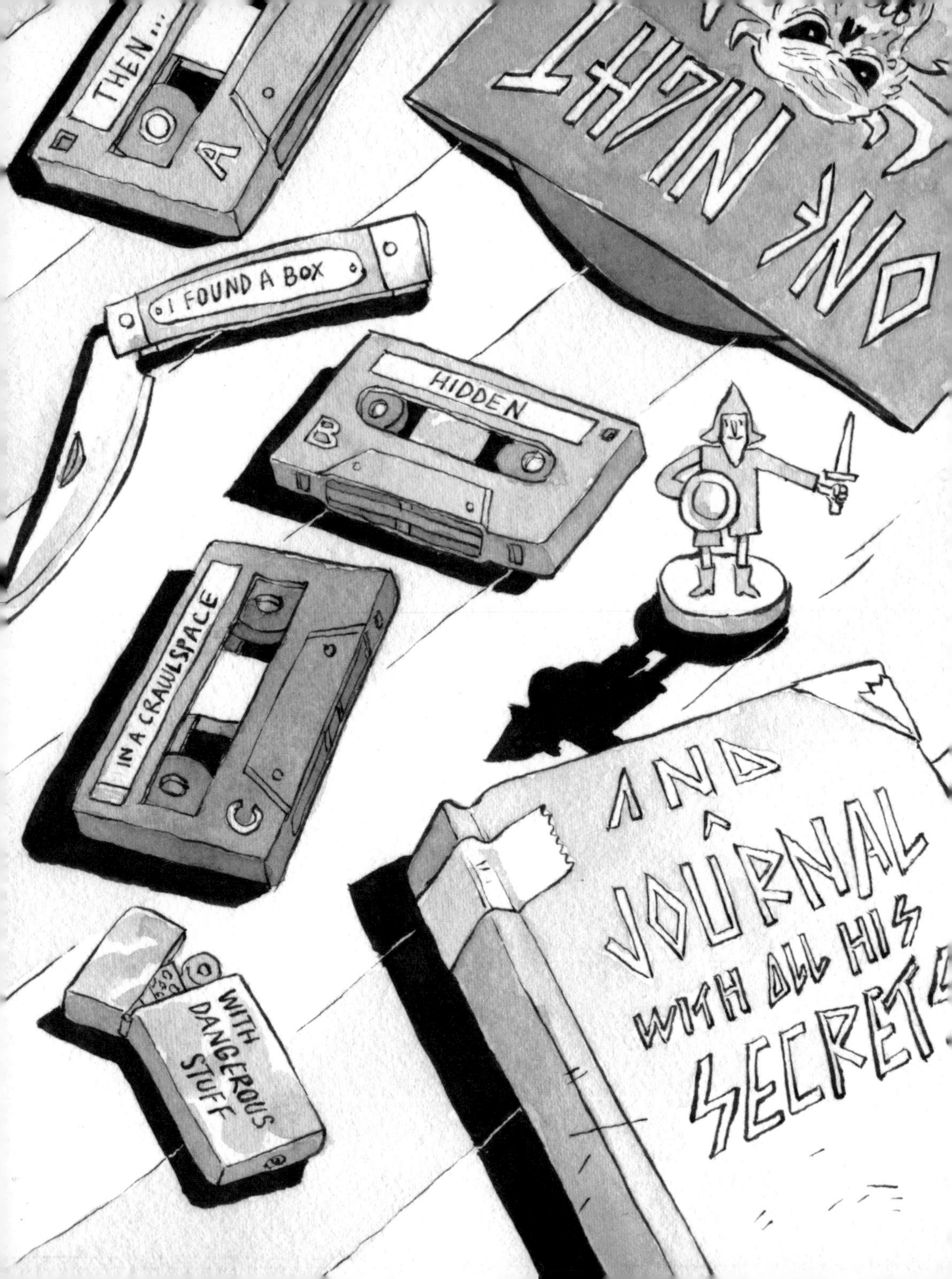
THEN...
I FOUND A BOX
HIDDEN
IN A CRAWLSPACE
WITH DANGEROUS STUFF
AND
JOURNAL
WITH ALL HIS
SECRET

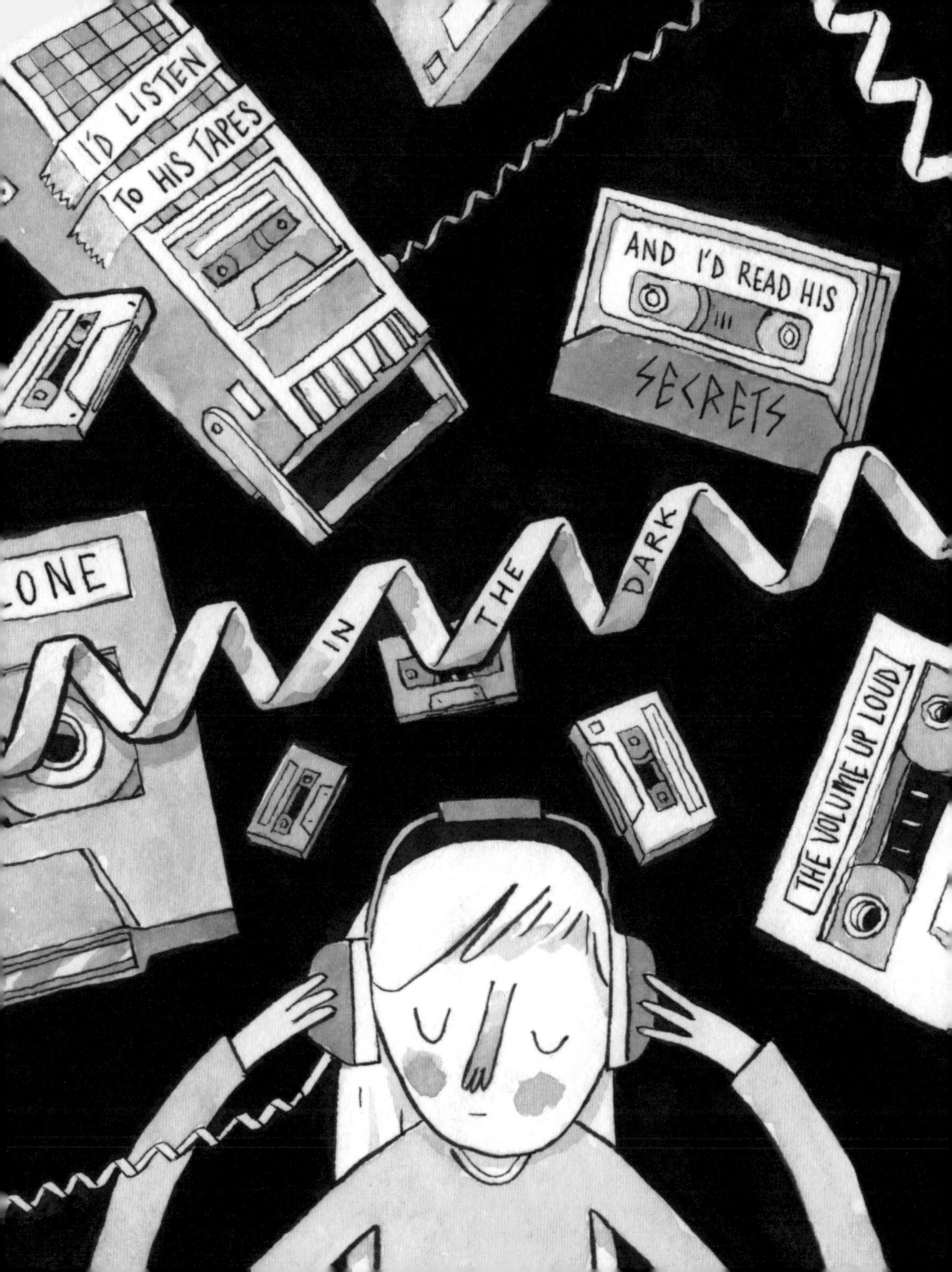

I'D LISTEN
TO HIS TAPES
AND I'D READ HIS
SECRETS
LONE
IN THE DARK
THE VOLUME UP LOUD

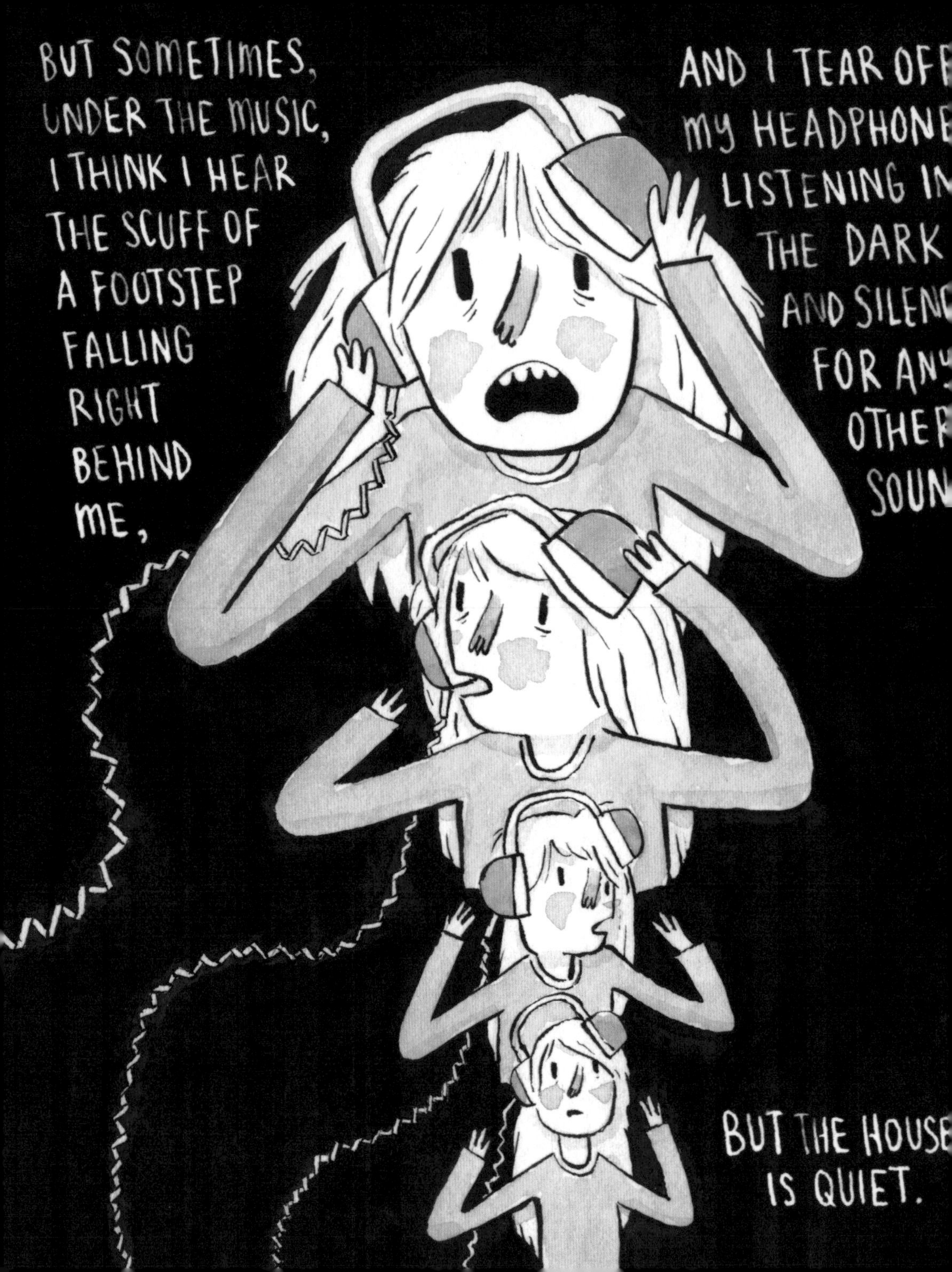
BUT SOMETIMES, UNDER THE MUSIC, I THINK I HEAR THE SCUFF OF A FOOTSTEP FALLING RIGHT BEHIND ME,
AND I TEAR OFF MY HEADPHONE LISTENING IN THE DARK AND SILENC FOR ANY OTHER SOUN
BUT THE HOUSE IS QUIET.

SLOWLY, AFTER MY HEART
STOPS RACING, I GET BACK
TO MY SECRETS.

THE
END.

FEAR #70

SOMETIMES I FORGET LITTLE THINGS,

AND I WORRY MY MIND IS DRIFTING AWAY FROM ME.

FEAR # 71

WHEN MY FEET ARE UP ON THE COFFEE TABLE,

AND A FRIEND WALKS IN,

I WORRY THEY'LL TRIP,

AND MY KNEES WILL BREAK BACKWARD.

FEAR # 72

I FEEL LIKE I'LL DIE OF OLD AGE SOME DAY,

AND RIGHT AFTER I'M GONE,

SOMETHING AMAZING WILL BE INVENTED,

AND I'LL TOTALLY MISS OUT.

FEAR #73

WHEN I PEEL POTATOES,

I WORRY THAT THEY FEEL PAIN THE WHOLE TIME,

BUT THEIR SCREAMS ARE TOO HIGH-FREQUENCY,

SO I NEVER HEAR A THING.

FEAR # 74

I ASKED MY PARENTS WHY I COULD NEVER REMEMBER THE MOMENT I FELL ASLEEP.

THEY TOLD ME IT'S BECAUSE I AM A CYBORG THAT THEY SHUT DOWN EACH NIGHT.

FEAR #75

IN A NIGHTMARE, I
WAKE UP ON A PLANE.

EVERYONE ELSE IS
ASLEEP. THE CREW,

AND THE PILOTS. I TRY TO YELL, TO WAKE THEM UP,

BUT NOTHING COMES OUT. EVERYTHING'S QUIET.

FEAR #76

MY GRANDMOTHER WOULD ALWAYS TELL ME:

"IF YOU FEEL A SHIVER ALONG YOUR SPINE,

SOMEWHERE,

SOMEONE JUST WALKED ACROSS YOUR FUTURE GRAVE."

FEAR # 77

WHEN I PUT MY HAND OUT THE WINDOW TO FEEL THE BREEZE,

I WORRY A PASSING BIKER WILL GIVE ME A HIGH FIVE,

AND THE FORCE WILL TAKE OFF BOTH OUR ARMS.

FEAR # 78

A LONG TIME AGO, I WAS CAMPING WITH MY FAMILY.

I SAW SOME FIREFLIES OFF IN THE WOODS,

BUT MY MOTHER TOLD ME TO STAY AWAY.

THEY WERE THE EYES OF THE GHOSTS.

FEAR # 79

WHEN I FIND MYSELF IN
A NEW PLACE,

I ALWAYS MAKE A QUICK
MENTAL CALCULATION:

IF I WERE TO DIE
SUDDENLY,

HOW LONG TILL SOMEONE
FINDS MY BODY?

FEAR #80

I CAN'T SLEEP WHEN IT'S WINDY OUTSIDE.

THE BRANCHES RATTLE AND SCRAPE MY WINDOW.

IN MY HEAD, THE NOISES
BECOME LONG FINGERS

GROWING FROM LONG,
TWISTED ARMS.

FEAR #81

WHEN I PACK UP SOMETHING
TO TAKE TO THE POST OFFICE,

I WORRY MY PACKAGE WILL
SOMEHOW BE IN A CRIME SCENE,

AND THE FINGERPRINTS AND
CAT HAIR STUCK IN THE TAPE

WILL LEAD THE POLICE
STRAIGHT TO ME.

FEAR #82

MIRRORS ARE GATEWAYS

TO ANOTHER DIMENSION,

BUT SOMEONE IS ALWAYS

BLOCKING MY WAY.

FEAR #83

my COUNTRY HAS A SAYING: "IF A BED STAYS EMPTY,

EVENTUALLY A GHOST WILL MAKE IT THEIR OWN."

WHENEVER I COME HOME FROM COLLEGE,

I FEEL LIKE my ROOM IS NO LONGER my OWN.

FEAR #84

MY PARENTS TOLD ME,

IF I STAYED TOO LONG
IN THE BATH,

I WOULD GROW GILLS,

AND BECOME A FISH.

FEAR #85

WHEN I GET HOME
FROM WORK,

SOMETIMES I CATCH AN
UNFAMILIAR SCENT,

AND I WORRY THAT
SOMEONE USES MY HOUSE

WHILE I'M AWAY.

FEAR #86

I TRY NOT TO STAND
NEXT TO WINDOWS.

THAT WAY, IF GRAVITY
TURNS SIDEWAYS,

I'LL LAND SAFELY ON
A WALL.

I ALSO TRY TO WATCH
OUT FOR FURNITURE.

FRAN KRAUSE

FEAR #87

GOING TO MY DAD'S HOUSE FOR THE WEEKEND, WE'D DRIVE BY A SMALL AIRPORT AT NIGHT.

HE TOLD ME THE LIGHTS ON THE RUNWAY WERE FALLEN STARS. HE WAS TRYING TO BE SWEET, BUT IT MADE ME AFRAID OF STARS.

FEAR #88

I HAVE TWO KIDS.
I SECRETLY WORRY...

...THAT EVERY BABY IS BORN
WITH A GENIUS-LEVEL IQ,

BUT EACH TIME THEIR
HEAD GETS BUMPED,

THEY LOSE A LITTLE
BIT OF THEIR SMARTS.

FEAR #89

SOMETIMES I WEIGH
MYSELF BEFORE BED.

THEN, THE VERY NEXT
MORNING,

I FIND THAT I'VE
GAINED A POUND.

THAT'S A LOT
OF SPIDERS.

FEAR # 90

I DON'T LIKE USING AN
AIRPLANE BATHROOM.

I WORRY WHEN I
FLUSH,

I'LL BE SUCKED INTO THE TOILET AND SHOT OUT OF THE PLANE.

FEAR # 91

WHEN THE DENTIST
NUMBS MY MOUTH,

I NEED TO BE VERY
CAREFUL.

I LOSE ALL FEELING
IN MY LIPS,

AND I WOULDN'T WANT TO
ACCIDENTALLY EAT THEM.

FEAR # 92

I'M AFRAID OF THE DARK, BUT I CAN'T SLEEP WITH THE LIGHTS ON.

SO, I LEAVE THE HALLWAY LAMP ON,

AND I WATCH THE SPACE UNDER MY DOOR.

THAT WAY, I'LL KNOW IF THERE'S A KILLER IN THE HALL,

OR A BLOOD-EYED CAT,

OR HUNDREDS OF THOUSANDS OF SPIDERS,

OR SOMETHING REALLY BIG,

OR A LITTLE GIRL WITH BLACK EYES FLOATING THREE FEET OFF THE GROUND.

FEAR #93

I'VE NEVER MET MY
BEST FRIEND.

WE ONLY TALK ONLINE.

I WORRY THAT SOME DAY
THEIR MESSAGES WILL STOP,

AND I'LL NEVER KNOW
WHY.

FEAR #94

WHEN THE LIGHTS IN MY HOUSE FLICKER AT NIGHT,

I WORRY IT'S GHOSTS SPEAKING IN MORSE CODE.

FEAR #95

SOMETIMES PEOPLE CAN BE SO MEAN TO EACH OTHER.

IT MAKES ME FEEL LIKE EVERYONE'S A MONSTER.

I HOPE I CAN BE THE KIND THAT FIGHTS AGAINST ITS NATURE

AND DOESN'T END UP EATING ANYONE.

FEAR # 96

WHEN I TAKE CARE OF MY HORSE, I OPEN UP TO HER,

AND I TELL HER EVERYTHING THAT'S ON MY MIND.

I WORRY, WHEN I'M NOT AROUND,

SHE TELLS ALL MY SECRETS.

FEAR # 97

ALL THE UNIVERSE IS JUST A DREAM IN GOD'S MIND,

IT'LL ALL DISAPPEAR IF HE EVER WAKES UP.

ABOUT THE AUTHOR

FRAN KRAUSE WAS BORN IN UPSTATE NEW YORK
BUT NOW LIVES IN LOS ANGELES WITH
HIS WIFE, JOANNA, AND A CAT NAMED CAT CAT.
HE TEACHES ANIMATION AT CALARTS AND LIKES
DRAWING COMICS AND RIDING HIS BIKE.

ACKNOWLEDGMENTS

FOR my mom, WHO ALWAYS TELLS ME GOOD STORIES.
THANK YOU KAITLIN KETCHUM AND
BETSY STROMBERG AT TEN SPEED PRESS.
I'D LIKE TO EXTEND MY THANKS TO EVERYONE
WHO SHARED THEIR STORIES AND FEARS WITH ME.

THANKS, EVERYBODY!

TO EVERYONE WHO SHARED THEIR FEARS WITH ME . . .

FEAR #1 - ANONYMOUS, #2 - ANONYMOUS, #3 - DOT,
#4 - ANONYMOUS, #5 - CLAIRE + KARISSA, #6 - JENNIFER,
#7 - ANONYMOUS, #8 - BERNARD, #9 - ANONYMOUS,
#10 - ANONYMOUS, #11 - JOANNA, #12 - VICTOR, #13 - VALERIA,
#14 - JANELLE, #15 - SHELBY, #16 - ANNIE, #17 - AAGAAP,
#18 - NICOLE, #19 - ANONYMOUS, THE BRIDGE - ANONYMOUS,
FEAR #20 - MARKABLOGS, #21 - M, #22 - ANDREA, #23 - JACQUI,
#24 - EFFY, #25 - ELLIE, #26 - DANAJ-B, #27 - MARGIE,
#28 - ANONYMOUS, #29 - AMANDA, #30 - ANONYMOUS,
#31 - EDDY, #32 - ANONYMOUS, #33 - KEHDI,
#34 - ANONYMOUS, #35 - EMMA, #36 - MEGAN, #37 - WALLIS,
#38 - SIMON, #39 - ANONYMOUS, #40 - KATE, #41 - DOMINIQUE,
#42 - ALEX, #43 - ANONYMOUS, #44 - HECTOR, #45 - ANONYMOUS,
#46 - REX, #47 - ANONYMOUS, #48 - ANONYMOUS, #49 - HANNAH,
#50 - ANONYMOUS, #51 - MING, #52 - BRUNA, #53 - BOBBI,
#54 - M SZ., #55 - ANONYMOUS, #56 - MAREK, #57 - ANONYMOUS,
#58 - ANONYMOUS, #59 - WEDNESDAY N, #60 - ANONYMOUS,
#61 - NOAH, #62 - CASEY, #63 - ANONYMOUS, #64 - LIZ,
#65 - ANGELA, #66 - SKYLER, #67 - MACLEFAME, #68 - CARLEIGH,
#69 - MEGAN, MY ATTIC ROOM - THE AMAZING AMARE,
FEAR #70 - ANONYMOUS, #71 - CHRISTOPHER, #72 - ANONYMOUS,
#73 - ANONYMOUS, #74 - ABBIE, #75 - BRENDAN, #76 - ANONYMOUS,
#77 - ANONYMOUS, #78 - ANONYMOUS, #79 - ANONYMOUS,
#80 - WHATWILLISWASTALKINBOUT, #81 - COURA, #82 - MURIELLE,
#83 - SUE, #84 - ZAN, #85 - MARIKA, #86 - JOE, #87 - HALEY,
#88 - MICHAELCTHULHU, #89 - MIKE, #90 - THANKSEARTHQUAKE,
#91 - BEN, #92 - ANONYMOUS, #93 - ANONYMOUS,
#94 - ANONYMOUS, #95 - ANONYMOUS, #96 - CATE, #97 - PAUL

THANK YOU ALL!

COPYRIGHT © 2017 BY FRAN KRAUSE

ALL RIGHTS RESERVED.
PUBLISHED IN THE UNITED STATES BY TEN SPEED PRESS,
AN IMPRINT OF THE CROWN PUBLISHING GROUP, A DIVISION
OF PENGUIN RANDOM HOUSE LLC, NEW YORK.
WWW.CROWNPUBLISHING.COM
WWW.TENSPEED.COM

TEN SPEED PRESS AND THE TEN SPEED PRESS COLOPHON ARE
REGISTERED TRADEMARKS OF PENGUIN RANDOM HOUSE LLC.

SOME COMICS APPEARED IN SLIGHTLY DIFFERENT FORM
ON DEEPDARKFEARS.COM.

LIBRARY OF CONGRESS CATALOGING-IN-PUBLICATION DATA
IS ON FILE WITH THE PUBLISHER.

HARDCOVER ISBN: 978-0-399-57914-1
EBOOK ISBN: 978-0-399-57915-8

PRINTED IN CHINA

DESIGN BY BETSY STROMBERG

10 9 8 7 6 5 4 3 2 1

FIRST EDITION

ANNIE

The Gorilla
Nanny

For Megan Larkin
J. W.

For the van Os Family, Klub Barbounia members
K. P.

www.korkypaul.com

ORCHARD BOOKS
96 Leonard Street, London EC2A 4XD
Orchard Books Australia
32/45-51 Huntley Street, Alexandria, NSW 2015
ISBN 1 84362 147 9 (hardback)
ISBN 1 84362 155 X (paperback)
First published in Great Britain in 2004
First paperback publication in 2005
Text © Jeanne Willis 2004
Illustrations © Korky Paul 2004
The rights of Jeanne Willis to be identified as the author
and of Korky Paul to be identified as the illustrator of this
work have been asserted by them in accordance with the
Copyright, Designs and Patents Act, 1988.
A CIP catalogue record for this book is available
from the British Library.
1 3 5 7 9 10 8 6 4 2 (hardback)
1 3 5 7 9 10 8 6 4 2 (paperback)
Printed in Great Britain

ANNIE

The Gorilla Nanny

Jeanne Willis * Korky Paul

ORCHARD BOOKS

ANNIE

The Gorilla Nanny

Hush now, children! Sit up straight!
Behave yourselves while I relate
My story. Stop that giggling, please,
Or I will have to slap your knees.

I've cared for tougher kids than you.
I trained on monkeys at the zoo.
I took my Nannying degree
In Gibbon and in Chimpanzee.

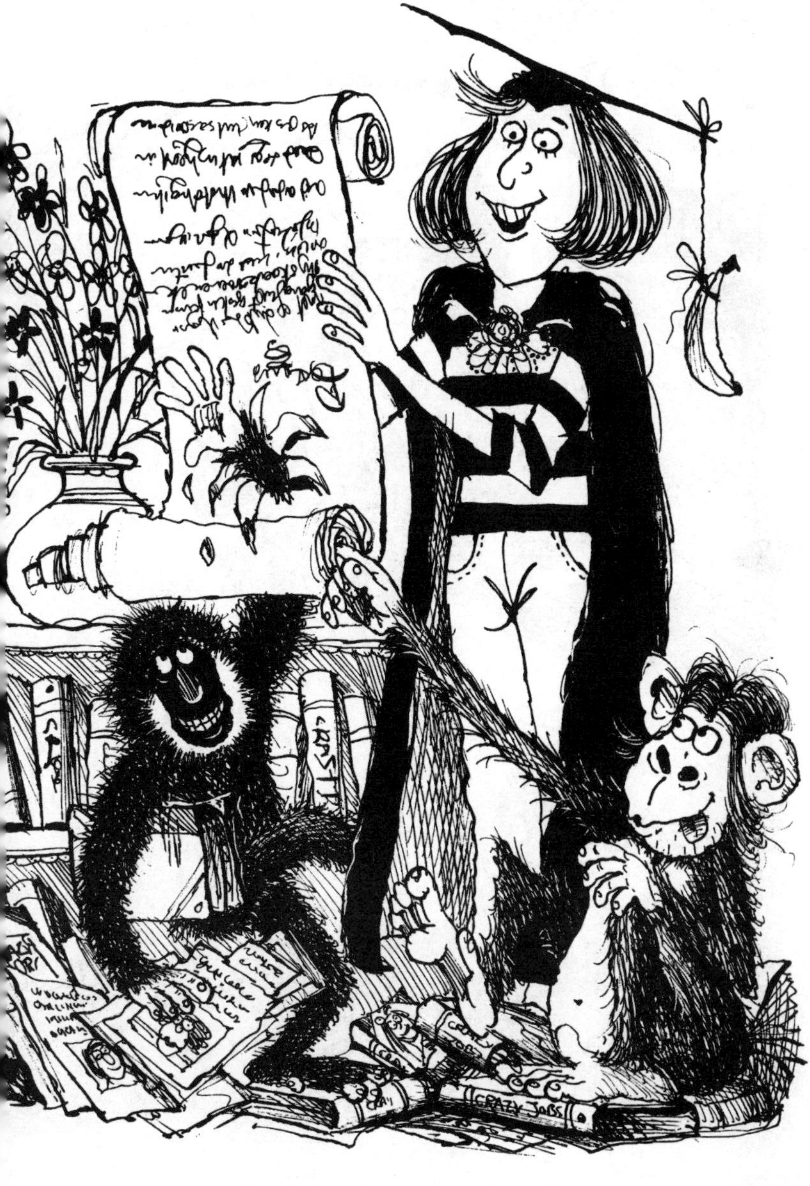
CRAZY JOBS

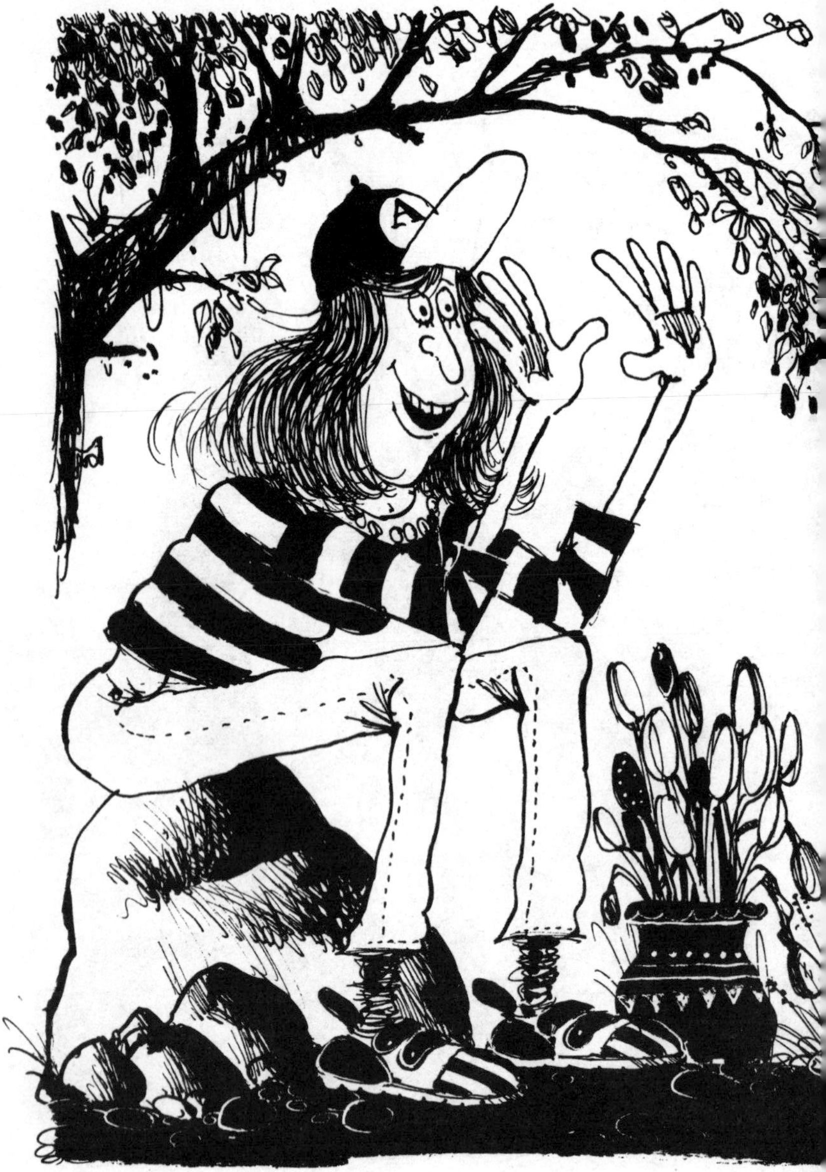

I've babysat for twin baboons -
I taught them how to eat with spoons,
And how to count from one to ten
Like perfect little gentlemen.

I nursed a young orang-utan.
Well, what a cheeky little man!
He didn't like the look of me
And blew a great big raspberry.

"Nanny won't have that!" I said,
And marched him straight upstairs to bed
Without his teddy or his tea.
(Look, no one makes an ape of me.)

My motto is, "Be firm but fair,"
With all the creatures in my care.
My famous clients don't complain.
I've glowing references from Jane...

...And Tarzan. Their adopted child
Was such a monkey! Running wild!
He wouldn't wash or walk or dress.
I'm not surprised, I must confess.

I blame the parents. Dearie me,
No discipline at all, you see?
They simply swung around on rope.
I swear they'd never heard of soap.

I said to Tarzan, "Wear a shirt!
A pair of trousers wouldn't hurt!
If you wander in the nude,
Your toddler's bound to turn out rude."

I spoke to Jane, I said to her,
"You can't complain of sticky fur,
Or that your boy won't wash his face,
Look at your hair! It's a disgrace."

"Might I suggest a curly perm?"
(I told you I was fair but firm.)
I taught Jane how to clean and cook
And how to read my ape-care book.

Job done, I left their nursery.
They sent a charming card to me:
Dear Annie, thanks to your advice
Our lad is well-behaved and nice.

P.S. Instead of wrestling crocs,
Tarzan washes pants and socks
And helps around the treehouse too!
Love Jane. (P.P.S Thanks to you!)

Their letter came by pigeon post
(So full of praise!). I hate to boast
But in this notelet, at the end,
They asked if I could help a friend.

This friend was not just anyone -
He was the King of Tongistan
And could I meet him Monday night?
(Enclosed: A ticket for my flight.)

I was greeted by the King
And this little hairy thing,
Which kept on jumping up and down
And snatching off his royal crown.

"I bought him for the Queen of France,"
The King said. "There's a Dinner-Dance
In honour of her birthday, she
Is going to be ninety-three!"

The Queen, it seemed, collected apes
Of several different sorts and shapes.
The King had heard that it would thrill her
To receive a young gorilla.

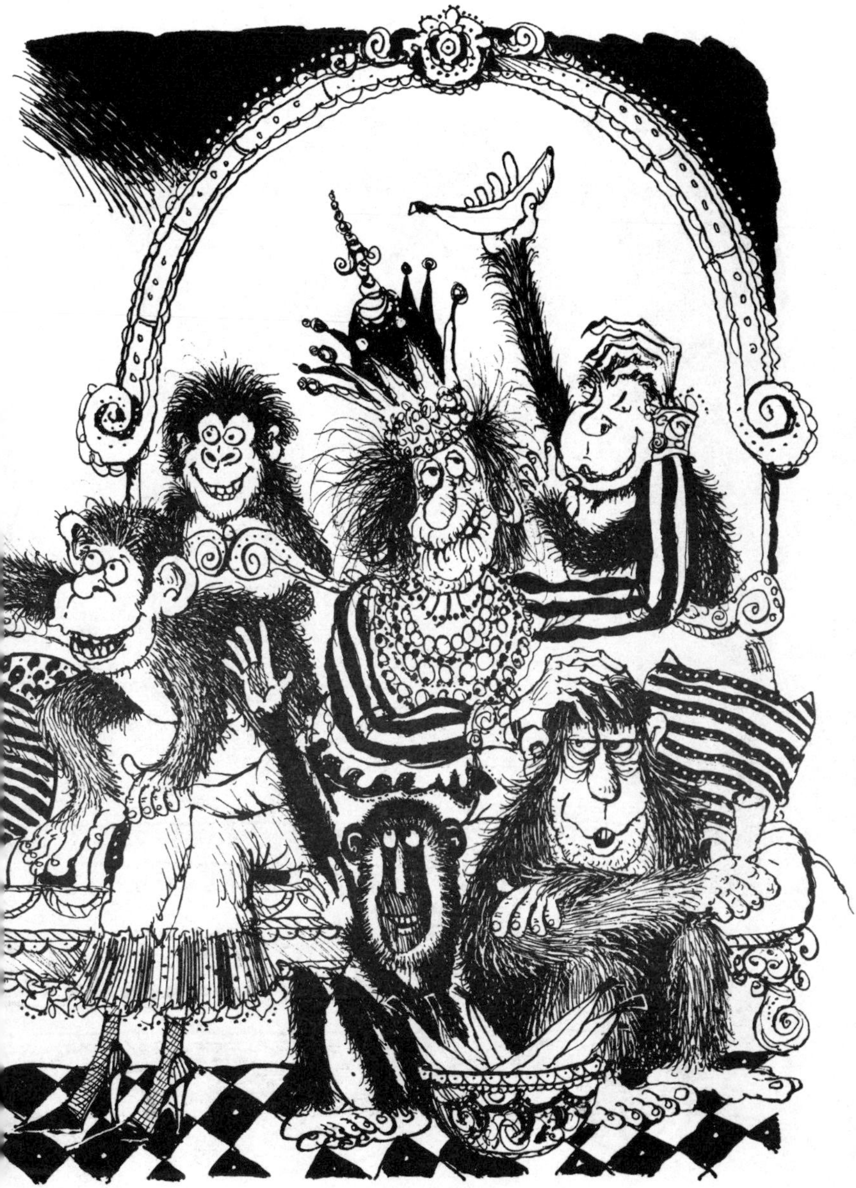

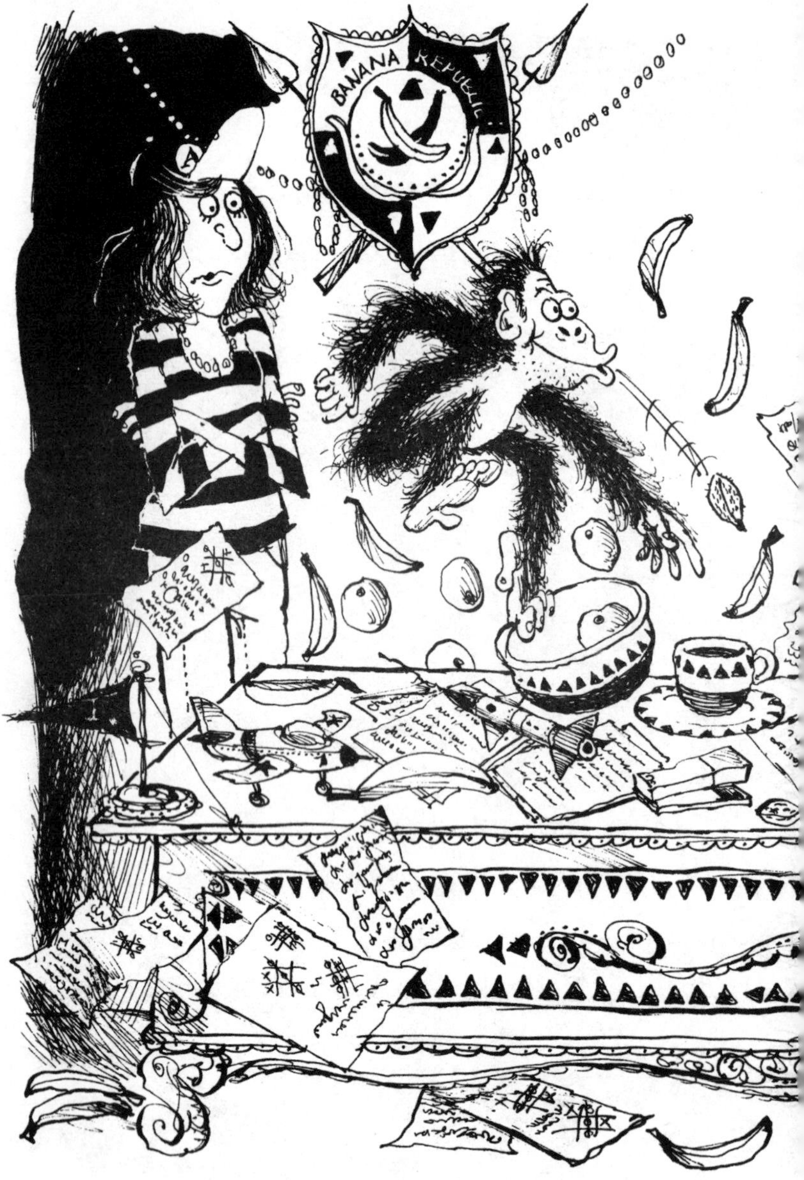
BANANA REPUBLIC

"But it throws coconuts!" he said,
"One hit my servant on the head.
It swears, it scratches and it screeches.
And it spits the stones from peaches!"

"This primate needs some proper training,
Or the Queen will write, complaining
That its manners are precocious
And its attitude's atrocious!"

"Do not fret, your Majesty,"
I curtseyed, "Give the ape to me!
With tough-love and a good routine
I'll have him fit to meet the Queen."

I held it gently by the hand
And said, "Now, dearie, understand
That you must do as I request –
You know that Nanny knows what's best."

"Don't pick your nose, it isn't nice!
Don't scratch your fleas or eat your lice.
Don't stick your bottom in the air
And don't pull faces, strings or hair."

"Don't beat chests, shake hands instead!
Don't suck your toes, it makes them red.
Don't slurp your tea or lick your plate,
Just smile politely, sit and wait."

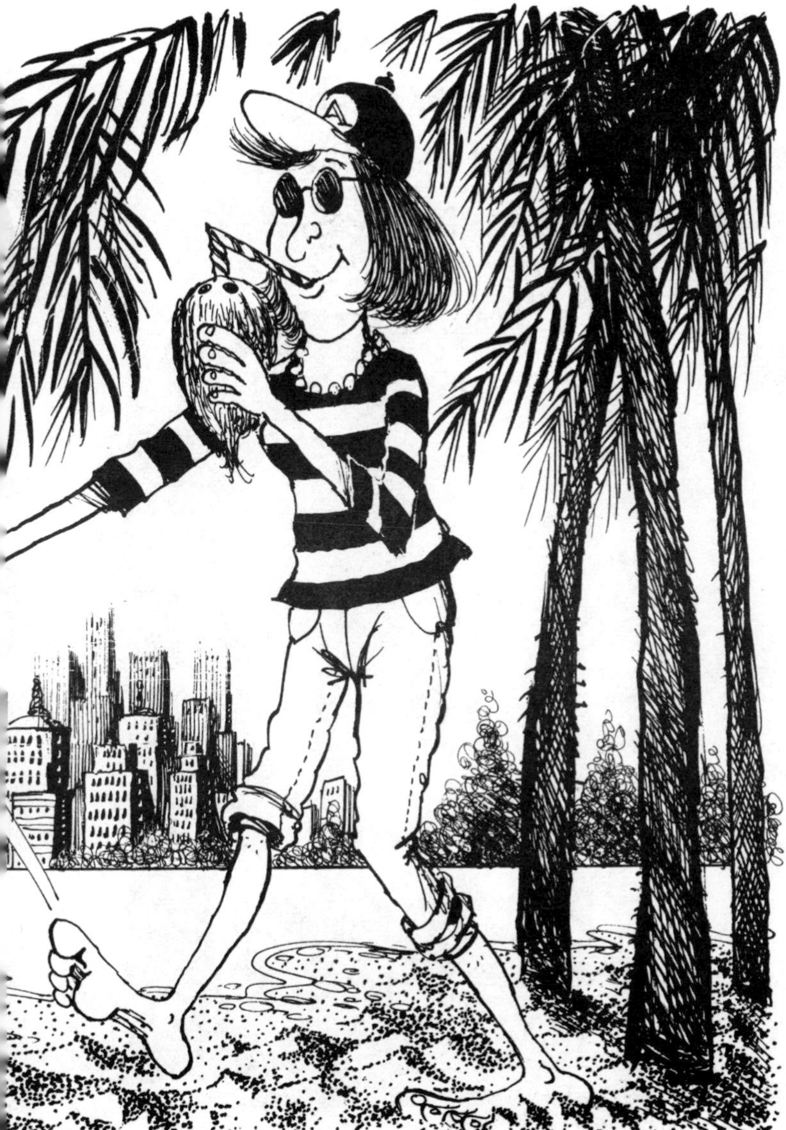

The little chap was good as gold -
He always did as he was told.
He gave his seat up on the bus
And combed his fur without a fuss.

He learnt to do his ABC
And he recited poetry.
Soon he could dance like Fred Astaire
And always wore clean underwear.

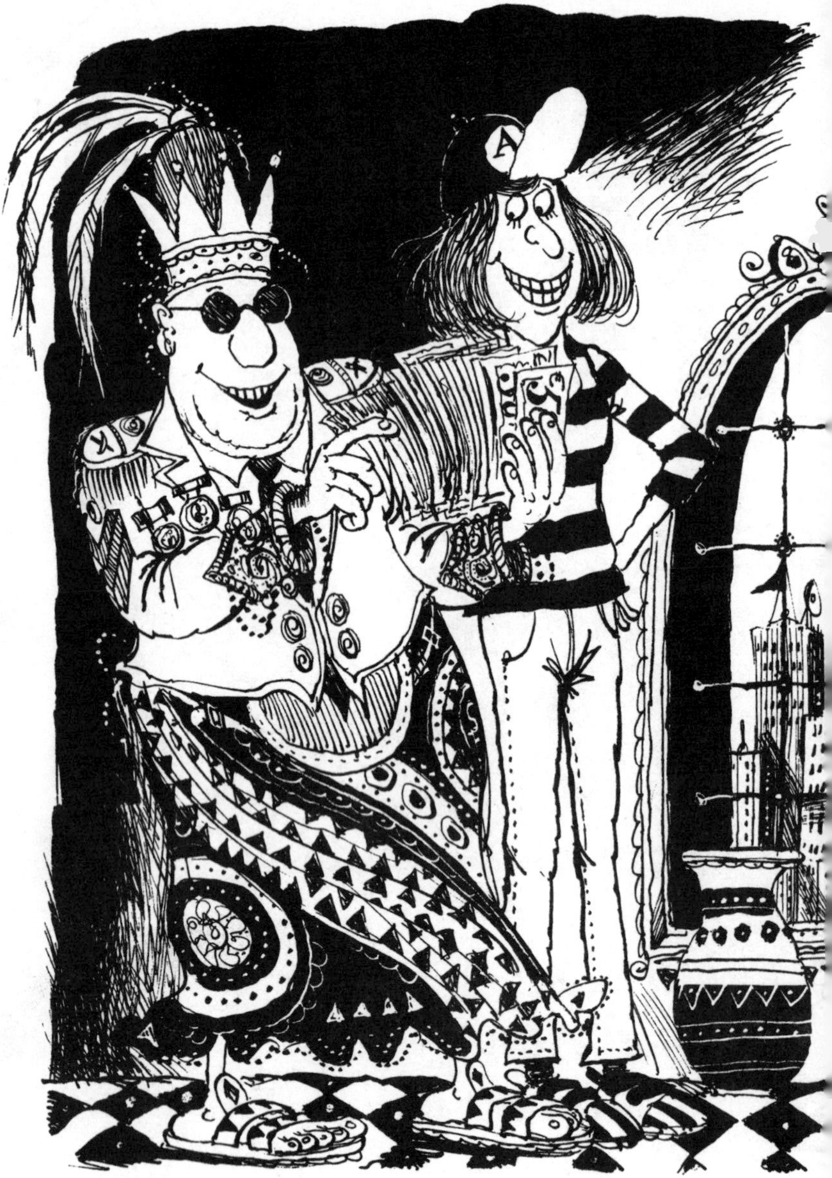

The King was thrilled. (I got a rise.)
The Queen cried, "What a sweet surprise.
What perfect manners! Oh, well done!
He's so much nicer than my son!"

37

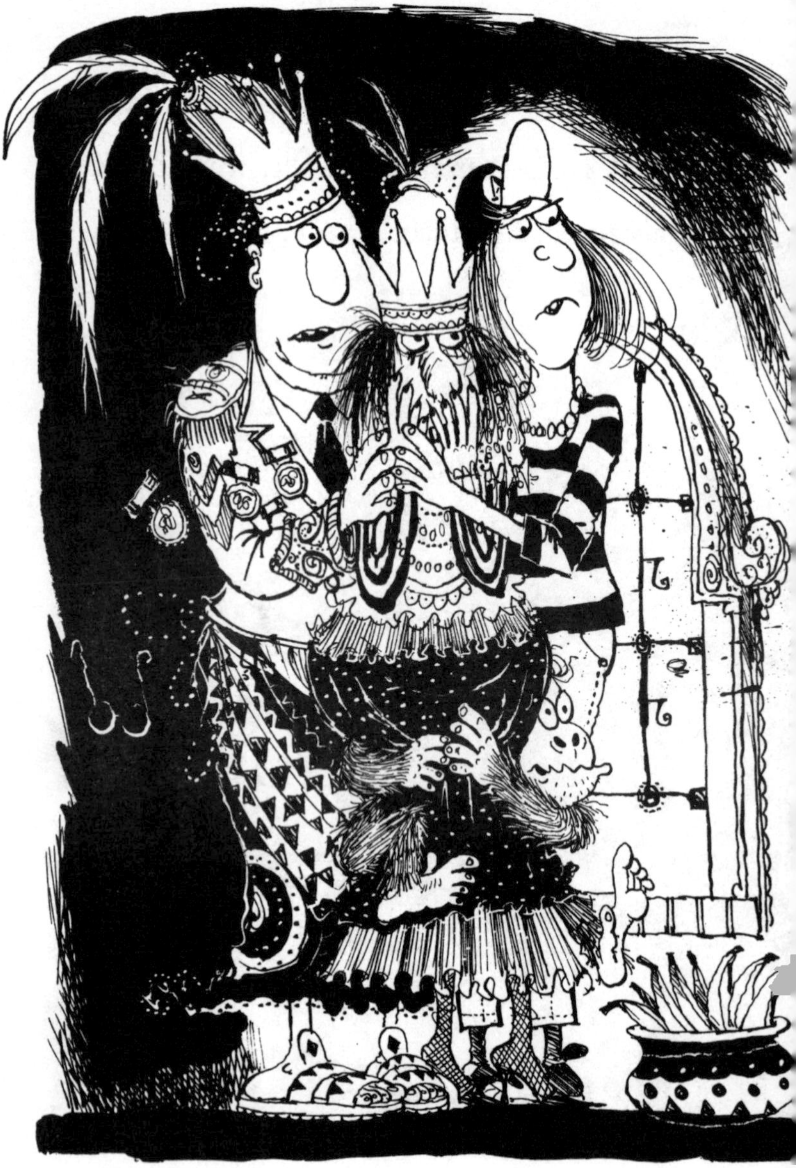

The prince stuck out his tongue and said,
"Naff off, Queenie. When you're dead,
Then I'll be King, make no mistake!"
He sprayed out crumbs of birthday cake.

How wrong he was! For when she died
The people of that country cried,
"Down with the Prince, he'll not be King,
The nasty, rude, ill-mannered thing!"

"Crown our Gorilla, wise and good –
He never spits out bits of food
Or pulls horrid, silly faces
(Or breaks wind in public places)."

41

They made him King! By his decree
The best bananas would be free.
The children could make nests in trees
And ladies could have hairy knees.

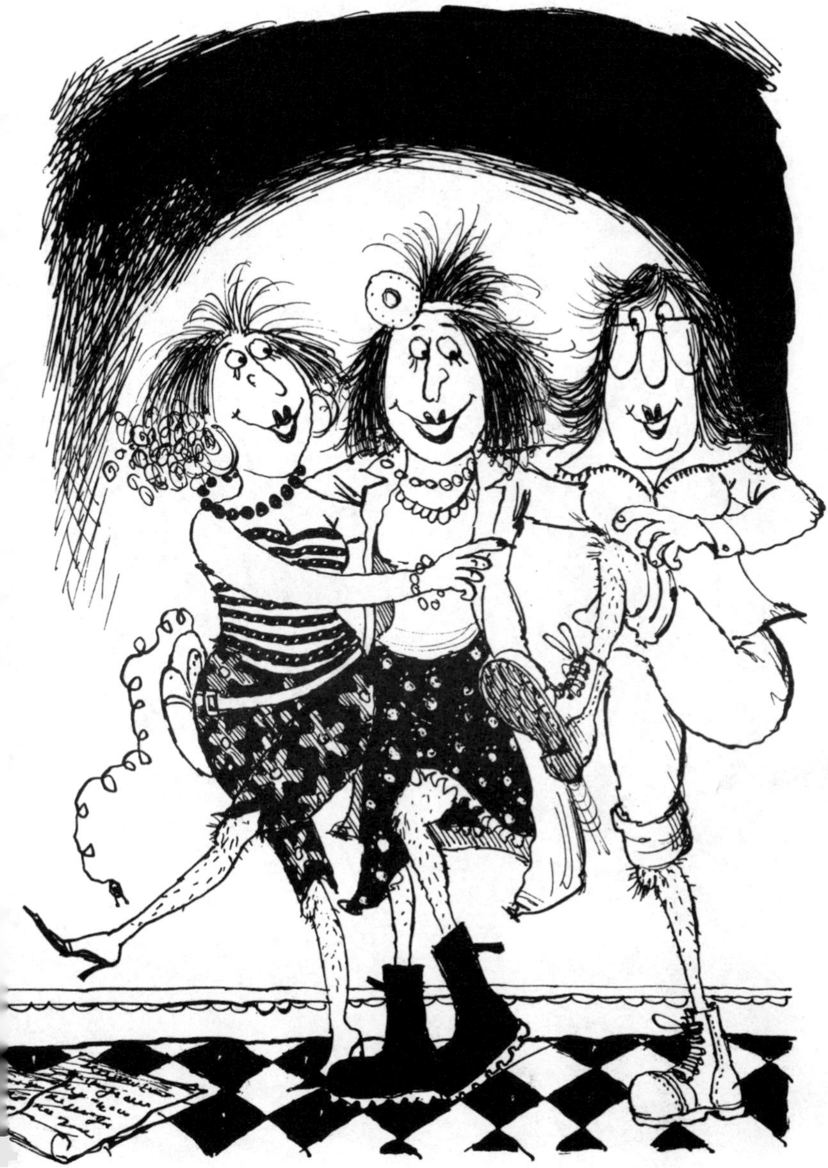

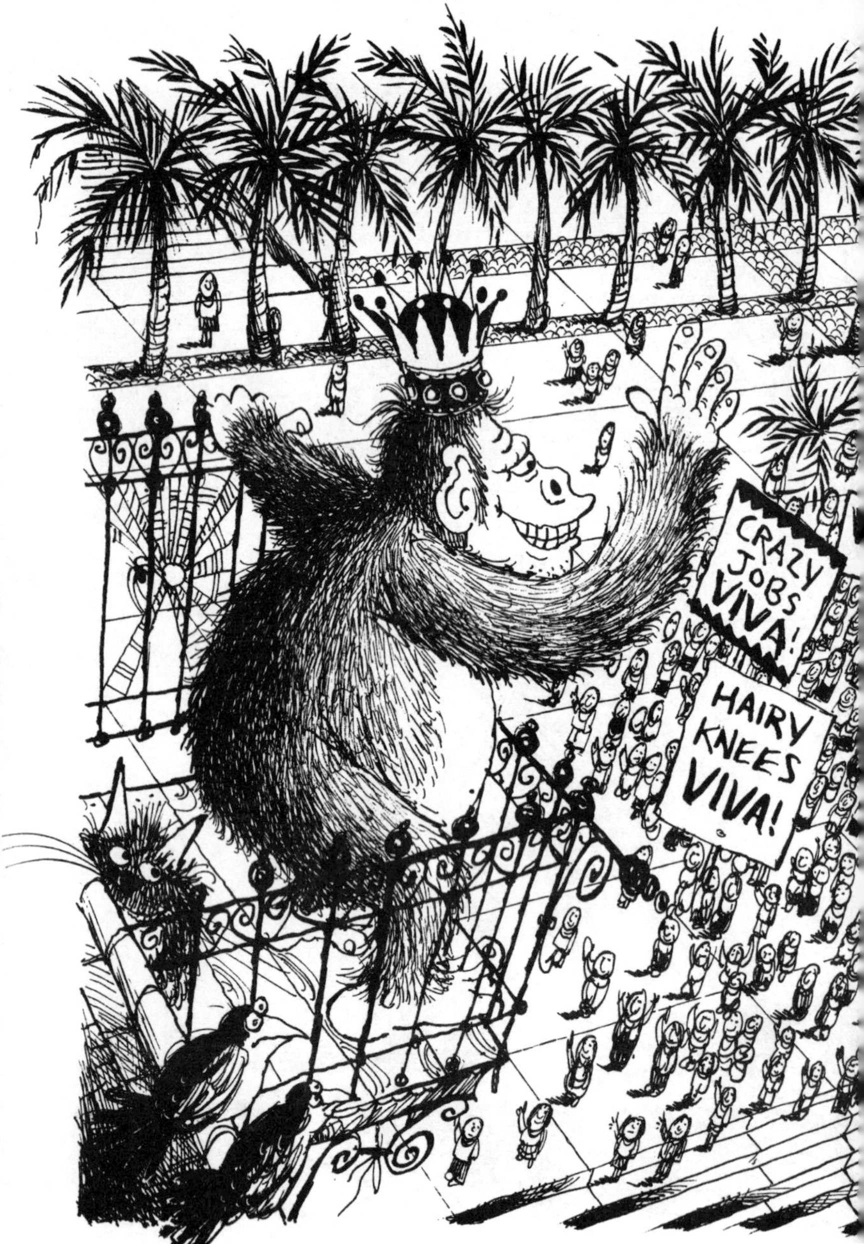
CRAZY JOBS VIVA!
HAIRY KNEES VIVA!

His loyal subjects love him so.

Which really only goes to show

That if you're brought up properly,

You're just as good as royalty.

I'll stay with the King for the rest of his life.
I went to his wedding! (I found him a wife.)
She gave me a job at their palace address...
In charge of the baby Gorilla Princess!

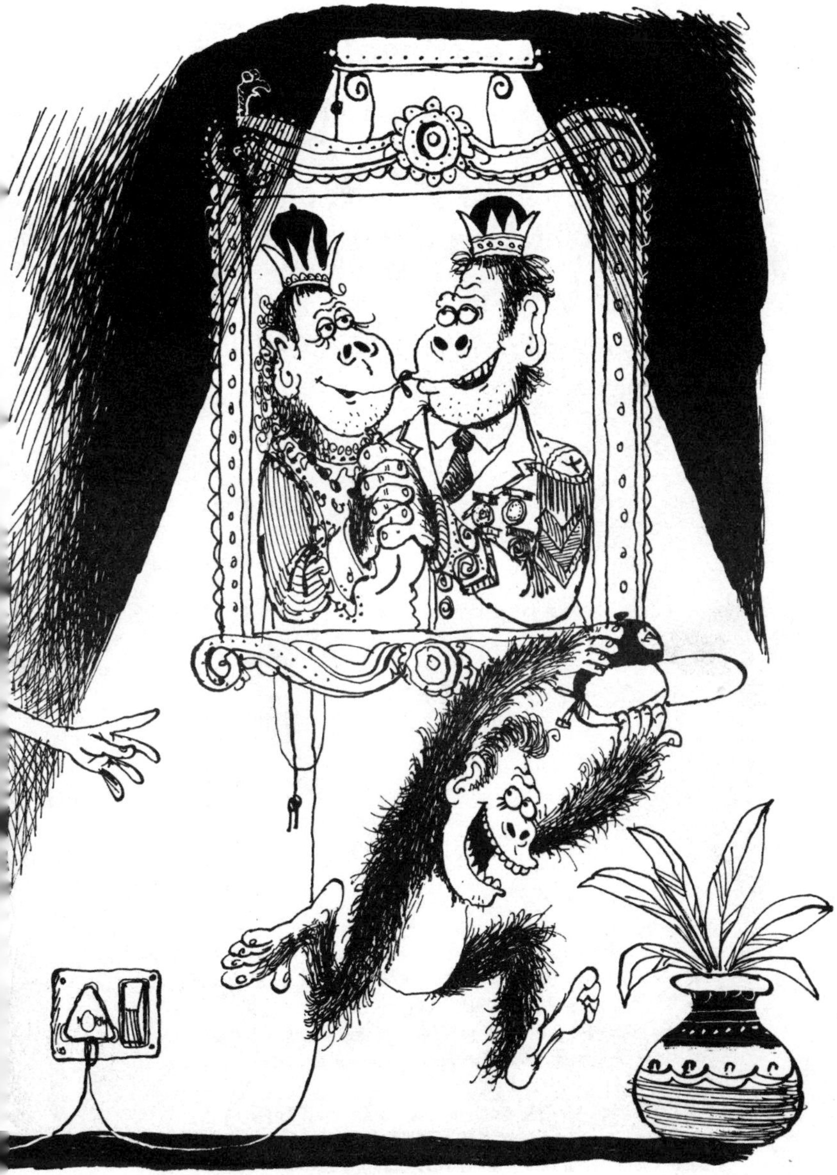

Written by Jeanne Willis * Illustrated by Korky Paul

All priced at £3.99 each

Crazy Jobs are available from all good book shops, or can be ordered direct
from the publisher: Orchard Books, PO BOX 29, Douglas IM99 1BQ
Credit card orders please telephone 01624 836000
or fax 01624 837033 or visit our Internet site: www.wattspub.co.uk
or e-mail: bookshop@enterprise.net for details.

To order please quote title, author and ISBN
and your full name and address.
Cheques and postal orders should be made payable to 'Bookpost plc.'
Postage and packing is FREE within the UK
(overseas customers should add £1.00 per book).
Prices and availability are subject to change.